MANAGING CURRICULUM AND ASSESSMENT

A Practitioner's Guide

Beverly Nichols

Sue Shidaker

Gene Johnson

Kevin Singer

Linworth Books

Professional Development Resources for K-12
Library Media and Technology Specialists

Library of Congress Cataloging-in-Publication Data

Nichols, Beverly
  Managing curriculum and assessment : a practitioner's guide / Beverly Nichols ... [et al.].
    p. cm.
  Includes bibliographical references (p.   ) and index.
  ISBN 1-58683-216-6 (pbk.)
  1. Curriculum planning. 2. Currriculum evaluation. I. Nichols, Beverly (Beverly W.) II. Title.
LB2806.15.M357 2006
375'.001--dc22

                              2006003202

Published by Linworth Publishing, Inc.
480 East Wilson Bridge Road, Suite L
Worthington, Ohio 43085

ISBN 1-58683-216-6

TABLE OF CONTENTS

TABLE OF FIGURES

PREFACE

Curriculum is an area of education that is characterized by a lack of agreement about its definition and nature. There are those who have divorced themselves completely from much curricular practice at all and want to talk about curriculum only as a discourse on politics and culture. These are mostly academians. And that dialogue can be a lively and interesting conversation. However, rarely does it ever get connected to the world in which most classroom teachers and administrators live and toil. When it comes to laws and expectations like those of *No Child Left Behind*, most academians have little to say except to condemn them as unwise laws. However, practitioners need advice on how to respond to such requirements, even those which may be based on fallacious assumptions about school effectiveness, in order to make the most and best of what is included for the children they are pledged and paid to serve.

This is a book by intelligent practitioners who have lived and worked in many school districts. Their view of curriculum practice is not mere technique, nor mindless sequencing of "magic steps" to minimally comply with laws and regulations. The authors are not "arm chair" advisors or distant consultants. Rather, they are thoughtful practitioners who have "walked the walk." And it just hasn't been an aimless walking about. Rather, the authors of this book have labored not only in school districts and schools in which they were employed as teachers and administrators, but also in countless others as curriculum auditors, curriculum leadership consultants, and subject area content experts. They know what it is to intervene in the daily affairs of schools and school systems. They have encountered the skeptics and the naysayers. They have persevered and have made a difference. Their book is a kind of passing of the torch of their learnings to others. Even if you think you know what they have done, just reading about it will provide some new insights you may not have considered before. It has been my pleasure to have worked with all of the authors as colleagues, so I know the educator who lives in each of them. Theirs is the kind of idealism that is respectful of the educational enterprise in which we all believe.

I was once told that the definition of "organizational love" was *disciplined caring*. These authors not only care deeply about schools, children, and learning, but they also have labored in the cause of organizational love, and they continue to do so in a disciplined way. What they have written is an example of the discipline that is necessary to be responsive to the curricular requirements confronting educators in these times.

Perhaps the highest tribute one colleague might pay to another is to note, as I do, that if my professional reputation were on the line for the curriculum/organizational study I had to do, these are the people I would want on my team. They are practical, tough-minded, and excellent teachers.

So open these pages with confidence. What these authors have to tell you they have done, and the practices work. There are, of course, many other things one could write about these days concerning curriculum. But the litmus test has been and will continue to be most important in the work place of classrooms and schools. If that is where you also toil, you will discover that this book is an invaluable resource.

– Fenwick W. English
R. Wendell Eaves Distinguished Professor of Educational Leadership
School of Education, University of North Carolina at Chapel Hill

INTRODUCTION

Suppose you want to travel with a large group of people from one side of the country to the other, starting and ending at the same time, while traveling in separate vehicles. Along the way you have certain locations at which you must meet at pre-determined times. How do you proceed?

You could tell everyone to get in their cars and head out, letting luck, chance, and individual talent determine your success. Or, you could plan your trip, creating a map and timeline that are feasible and checking progress along the way. While both methods might get you to your goal, only one will do it efficiently and effectively.

Guiding a large group of students from kindergarten through high school graduation is a similar journey. They can travel without a map, hoping that the talents of the drivers lead them in the most efficient, effective path. Or they can follow a sequential plan designed to maximize their use of time, align their learnings, and check their progress. Which idea can be replicated, and which one provides the most opportunity for success?

While traveling without a map in today's educational environment might be adventurous, it often comes at an expensive price. Duplicated services, curricular gaps, misaligned tasks, mismatched resources, and disparate achievement performance are all symptomatic of on-the-fly design. Each one creates an obstacle to learning for the student and a poor use of resources for the district. Today, the stakes are too high for success to be left to chance.

Across the United States there is increasing emphasis on high-stakes assessment, student learning standards established by states, and the needs of school districts to improve curriculum alignment with national, state, and local goals and expectations. Requirements of the federal *No Child Left Behind* law have increased the urgency of improving student performance, and educators are literally scrambling to determine how to meet those needs as expeditiously and effectively as possible. Teachers, library media specialists, and administrators have sought expertise in curriculum design, delivery, evaluation, and management, often with very limited financial and human resources upon which to draw during these efforts.

The purpose of this practitioners' handbook and the accompanying CD is to provide the basic elements of a curriculum management system that will help school districts address the need to improve student learning in as practical a manner as possible. The emphasis throughout the book on alignment of the written, taught, and tested curriculum provides a framework for quality control of a district's educational program. The guidance presented here draws heavily upon the foundations of curriculum management initiated and developed by Fenwick English. Further resources are the many school systems in which the authors have observed, trained, or coached educators or in which they have themselves worked to implement changes congruent with the guidance offered.

While many states have developed student learning standards and frameworks, most are not specific enough to provide clear and precise objectives for teaching and learning in the classroom. Thus it is imperative that local school districts develop curriculum that will support teachers' instructional efforts to provide students equal access to the learning implicit in state standards and the assessments through which students are to demonstrate the knowledge and skills learned.

The handbook is organized into three sections. Section I provides a general overview of the activities critical to the design, development, and subsequent management of an effective curriculum system. Section II addresses more specific steps that demonstrate how to carry out the activities described in Section I. For several of the actions, Section III offers sample documents and templates. The same samples and documents are included on the CD so that district practitioners will not have to recreate them. The handbook further contains a glossary of terms, a suggested reading list for use by educators, and information regarding professional backgrounds of the authors.

Possible uses of the handbook and CD are varied. For example, the overview (Section I) might be sufficient for expanding understanding of the basic elements of a sound curriculum system by board members, administrators, and teachers. The "how to" steps of Section II might be most helpful to individuals charged with specific roles in stages of curriculum design, delivery, evaluation, or management. Certainly those practitioners are the ones likely to find some of the Section III examples particularly useful.

SECTION I • THE BIG PICTURE

Introduction: Concepts and Fundamentals

Curriculum management planning is a comprehensive function intended to produce a system for effective design, development, implementation, and evaluation of a district's curriculum. The planning includes several stages of work and should be established and communicated in a comprehensive curriculum management policy with administrative procedures or a board-adopted plan to direct the processes.

Section I provides an introductory overview of the curriculum management planning function and its components. The intent is to offer a common foundation of understanding upon which district leaders and staff can create a system or modify an existing system to ensure effective design and delivery of curriculum and assessment operations and optimize student achievement. The basic elements of Section I include the following:

✔ A needs assessment
✔ A curriculum development/review cycle
✔ An assessment plan that incorporates state and district assessments of student learning correlated with state expectations and district curriculum
✔ Scope-and-sequence documents for curriculum areas
✔ Curriculum guides for teachers in all curriculum areas, including librarians and media specialists
✔ Instructional materials selection
✔ Design and development of assessments for curriculum
✔ Staff development to support stages of design, delivery, and evaluation of the curriculum, including effective use of data
✔ Curriculum monitoring processes for administrators and teachers
✔ Assessment implementation and data use
✔ Program evaluation for decision-making

Overview of Curriculum Management Planning

Effective school districts have systematic plans for managing the design and delivery of curriculum. The plans should be required by board policy and described in a curriculum management document. Often included is a philosophical statement that describes district expectations regarding the alignment of curriculum, instruction, and assessment; their match to state or national standards; and their support of the district mission and vision. Roles and responsibilities related to curriculum, instruction, and assessment are identified and assigned.

The curriculum management plan includes three major processes: needs assessment, planning and design, and implementation. Each process is broken down into the functions shown in Figure 1.1.

Figure 1.1
Process and Function in Curriculum Management

Process	Function
Needs Assessment	Needs assessment
Planning and Design	Curriculum development cycle Comprehensive assessment plan Scope and sequence development Curriculum guides Materials selection Assessment design and development
Implementation	Staff development and implementation Monitoring curriculum delivery Assessment implementation and use of data Program evaluation

The cyclical model for the process is shown in the diagram in Figure 1.2.

Figure 1.2
The Curriculum Management Model

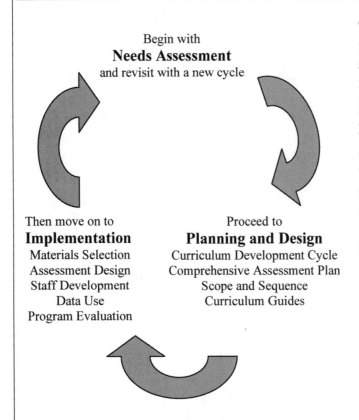

Begin with
Needs Assessment
and revisit with a new cycle

Then move on to
Implementation
Materials Selection
Assessment Design
Staff Development
Data Use
Program Evaluation

Proceed to
Planning and Design
Curriculum Development Cycle
Comprehensive Assessment Plan
Scope and Sequence
Curriculum Guides

The model shows that the process is cyclical and not linear. Needs assessment is an initial stage that identifies the various areas for improvement in the district. Planning and design follow. There are a number of functions that are completed in this stage. The planning and design phase represents the development of the district curriculum and is based on the items identified during the needs assessment. Finally, the most important stage of the cycle is the implementation phase or the delivery of the curriculum. It is in this stage that teaching and learning take place. It is also when assessment of the overall program is conducted. When complete, the assessment results feed into needs assessment for the continuation of the cycle.

Checkpoint for Curriculum Management Planning

1. What are the typical components of curriculum management planning?

2. Describe the cycle of processes involved in curriculum management planning.

3. Explain why each component of curriculum management planning is important.

Needs Assessment

Before launching a major curriculum development effort, school district leaders are advised to conduct a needs assessment to assist them in creating appropriate focus to the work. Improved student learning is always the goal sought, but aligning the written, taught, and tested curricula can reap many additional benefits: support for effective teaching, clarity of scope and sequence for student learning, and precision in linkage between specific learning objectives and the instructional materials and student assessments in use. To maximize the benefits of curriculum review, development, and evaluation, a needs assessment is the critical first step.

1. *What is a needs assessment in curriculum management?* The needs assessment considers the mission, purpose, and outcomes of the educational program and identifies any existing gaps between current status of student achievement and desired results. It reveals what is needed so that the organization can focus its efforts on changes that will support fulfillment of the district mission and purpose and attainment of the desired outcomes. A needs assessment may begin with strategic plan vision, purpose, and goal statements if such information is available and current. Otherwise, the quality of the needs assessment is strengthened by establishment of these premises before further action.

2. *Why is a needs assessment important?* A well-designed and effectively developed needs assessment provides the foundation upon which curriculum design and development will be built. Having a needs assessment in hand creates targeted focus for action and prevents unnecessary repetition of effort. The needs assessment identifies areas of concern based on quantitative data such as student test scores or qualitative data found in opinion surveys and staff discussions. Often, these data reflect shortcomings in written curriculum documents. These sources of information and feedback are the core elements of the assessment plan.

3. *Who conducts a needs assessment?* A needs assessment is led by a district administrator or staff member who is knowledgeable about data collection methods as well as the "big picture" of district curriculum and assessment responsibilities. An alternative guide to the needs assessment process is an external process expert with similar knowledge who can support the district administrative leaders and work effectively

with the organization's participants. Those who participate or contribute information during the needs assessment are typically:

- administrators,
- teachers,
- school library media specialists,
- students,
- parents or community members,
- state department of education staff, or
- intermediate educational unit staff (county, regional service districts).

4. *When is a needs assessment completed?* A needs assessment is completed before curriculum review and revision occur. (See Section I, Curriculum Development Cycle.) Timing during the year is dependent on when the curriculum review is scheduled to begin. Ensuring adequate time for completion and analysis before undertaking the review is the critical guideline on timing.

5. *How is a needs assessment conducted?* Conducting a needs assessment involves several specific steps. (See Section II, How to: Needs Assessment.) Most important is that the leadership for such a project possesses the skills of issue identification, question design, and inquiry format, as well as expertise in compiling and analyzing data for decision making. Communicating summary and disaggregated data and identifying implicit and explicit information from the data are other critical skills for the needs assessment leadership. The leadership can be internal or external, but credible and pertinent knowledge of both assessment strategies and organizational functions and responsibilities is most important.

With the results of a well organized and carefully implemented needs assessment, the district leaders and staff will be ready to move forward, making efficient and effective use of the time and energy committed to curriculum development. Data from the needs assessment provide part of the foundation for developing the scope and sequence and for conducting program evaluation.

Checkpoint for Needs Assessment

1. What is a needs assessment, and how does it contribute to effective curriculum planning and development?

2. What factors are typically considered in a comprehensive needs assessment that will assist curriculum developers in a school district?

3. Who leads and who participates in a needs assessment?

Curriculum Development Cycle

Schools exist for the purpose of teaching and learning. Too often school district personnel plan for issues that support teaching and learning—such as facilities, transportation, technology, and staff development—without developing a specific plan for creating the necessary foundation of curriculum. What knowledge and skills must students have to be successful in both an educational setting and the "real world" in which they live outside of school? This question is revisited in a timely and systematic fashion so that administrators, teachers, and librarians can provide the best learning opportunities possible for the students in their care.

1. *What is a curriculum development cycle?* A curriculum development cycle is a systematic schedule or calendar for addressing the design, delivery, and review of curriculum in all content areas. The timeline for the cycle includes both core and elective areas and is manageable within a district's human and financial resources. The components of the cycle include needs assessment, curriculum development or revision, materials selection, assessment development, and curriculum implementation. Implementation should include staff development and program evaluation for each content area.

2. *Why is a curriculum development cycle important?* Planning for curriculum development within a cycle allows district personnel to address ongoing curricular and instructional needs in a timely manner. The cycle provides for systematic allocation of resources so that financial resources can be budgeted wisely, and the capacity of district

staff members to assimilate new materials and perform required tasks will not be overloaded. Long-range budget planning can then anticipate and address all aspects of the curriculum development cycle.

3. ***Who establishes a curriculum development cycle?*** This task is ideally completed by personnel with knowledge of and responsibility for budget, resources, and curriculum. In larger districts, this would be a small committee comprised of central office personnel and representatives from the curriculum and instruction department, including media specialists. In smaller districts this might fall to a designated person with ancillary responsibilities in the curriculum area (e.g., assistant principal, lead teacher). Some districts choose to involve one or two representative parents or community members.

4. ***When does a curriculum development cycle begin and end?*** A complete cycle for all content areas covers a time period sufficiently long to include all core and elective subjects. A typical cycle for a given content area may cover a five- to seven-year span. In some states, a cycle might be determined by a state-mandated process for selecting new textbooks in a particular content area.

The table in Figure 1.3 is one example of a cycle that would cover the four core content areas.

Figure 1.3
A Sample Curriculum Development Cycle

	Needs Assessment	Curriculum Development	Materials Selection	Implementation	Program Evaluation
Math	Year 1	Year 2	Year 2	Year 3	Year 5
Lang. Arts	Year 2	Year 3	Year 3	Year 4	Year 6
Science	Year 3	Year 4	Year 4	Year 5	Year 7
Soc. St.	Year 4	Year 5	Year 5	Year 6	Year 8

A cycle like the one shown in Figure 1.3 would spread major textbook purchases across time, lessening the impact on budgets. Elementary school teachers who teach all subjects would not be expected to implement more than one new core curriculum in a given year.

Elective areas could be incorporated into the schedule above without a major effect on personnel or budgets; for example, mathematics and music could be done in one year, while science and physical education could be done in another. Development or revision of curriculum used by school librarians could occur simultaneously with work in language arts.

A "rule of thumb" has historically been that the number of curriculum groupings determines the length of the cycle. An eight-year cycle can have eight groupings. All subject areas must be included in the cycle. However, modification of this "rule of thumb" has become necessary in order for districts to establish cycles that correspond with state assessments, using the data for curriculum modification. Where state textbook adoptions have an established cycle that impacts local curriculum decisions, that schedule is also a guide to determining local cycles. The textbook is *not* the curriculum, but local planning must coincide with state adoptions in some instances.

Curriculum development includes building a scope and sequence and writing curriculum guides. Because work in other stages has an impact on the content of final curriculum documents, work does not move through the steps in a linear fashion.

If an eight-year cycle were to be instituted for each subject area, there would be some "down time" between program evaluation and needs assessment; however, data from the program evaluation would be a major component of the needs assessment at the beginning of a new cycle, as the student performance data would be.

5. *How is the cycle developed?* Initial development of the cycle will be influenced by several factors, such as existing state cycles for revision or textbooks adoption, national standards revision, available financial resources, student assessment performance, and capacity of district personnel to do the work. Once the initial cycle is developed, it is revisited periodically so that plans can be adjusted to meet changing circumstances.

Checkpoint for Curriculum Development Cycle

1. What are the factors that influence a district's determination of a curriculum development cycle?

2. When does a cycle begin and end—with what actions or products?

Comprehensive Assessment Plan

Some classroom teachers plan their assessments after a complete unit of instruction has taken place. A more effective practice is to include assessment as part of the overall unit plan before instruction begins. The same holds true for development of an aligned written, taught, and tested curriculum. Consideration of assessment needs is a vital part of the curriculum development process. What will a district assessment process look like? What types of assessments will be considered so there will be multiple measures of student learning? Will all objectives be included in district assessments, or will some objectives be more important than others? How will the assessments for a specific content area fit into a larger picture of district-wide assessments?

1. *What is a comprehensive, district-wide assessment plan?* A district-wide student assessment plan includes both high-stakes external assessments and local summative and formative assessments that test students at regular intervals throughout the year. The district plan will address the purpose for assessments, the scope of district assessments, plans for data collection and interpretation, and the expectation that data will be available and used for decision-making in a variety of ways, including needs assessment and program evaluation. Plans for data interpretation will address training or staff development for all stakeholders who will be analyzing and using data: school board members, administrators, teachers, media specialists, and parents. Likewise, the staff development needs of district personnel who will write local assessments need to be considered in the district-wide assessment plan.

2. *Why is a district assessment plan necessary?* A district's progress is publicly measured by high-stakes external assessments. With the enactment of *No Child Left Behind* legislation, these assessments are frequently the state tests on which Adequate Yearly Progress is based. Analysis of the data from once-a-year summative assessments and modification of curriculum and instruction based on the analysis is an important part of a district's assessment plan. However, a once-a-year summative assessment is "too little, too late" to have a positive impact on student achievement. Information about student learning is needed on a timely, ongoing basis throughout the year so that teachers can re-teach an objective to an entire class or work one-on-one with specific students so that all students master the desired learning. Based on assessment data, librarians can also provide additional support in those content areas where media use has been incorporated into the curriculum. The assessments used are

the means for answering the question: How will we know the students have learned what the curriculum intends them to learn?

3. ***Who creates a district assessment plan?*** A district-wide assessment plan is typically created by a team composed of central office personnel and building administrators. The team's membership includes the person who has responsibility for assessment and representatives from administrators and teachers who have responsibility for curriculum and instruction as well as assessment. Once district-wide needs for scoring and reporting have been identified, the district's manager of information systems can assist the planning team in determining the district technology support required to meet those needs. Planning content-specific assessments that are a part of the bigger picture will be a joint responsibility of district leadership and members of the curriculum development team for the content area.

4. ***When is a district assessment plan developed?*** Because a district assessment plan is the umbrella for development of content-area assessments, creation of the district-wide plan precedes the work of curriculum and assessment writing in any content area. Ideally, a district's curriculum management plan and the comprehensive assessment plan will be developed in conjunction with one another so the plans are cohesive and reflect district policies related to alignment of the written and tested curriculum.

5. ***How is a district assessment plan developed?*** The first step in developing a district assessment plan is selection of a team to do the work, as described in Step #3. Then a timeline for completing the task is established. A district assessment plan considers both mandated external assessments and district-wide assessments and the role each plays in improving student and district performance and accountability. The plan also addresses the components listed in #1 on page 13 (What is a district-wide assessment plan?). A calendar for external and district-wide assessments is developed so that assessments can be spaced throughout the year. The starting point for such a calendar is a complete listing of assessments to be administered, as illustrated in Figure 1.4. Once the plan is completed, it is presented to the board of education for approval. The following overview summarizes a sample district assessment plan.

Figure 1.4
Overview of District Assessments
XYZ School District

	K	1	2	3	4	5	6	7	8	9	10	11	12
Diagnostic Reading Assessment	X	X	X										
District Math (quarterly)				X	X	X	X	X	X				
District ELA (quarterly)				X	X	X	X	X	X				
District End-of-Course, 4 core areas										X	X	X	X
State Math Assessment				X	X	X	X	X	X	X			
State ELA Assessment				X	X	X	X	X	X	X			
State Science Assessment						X			X		X		
PSAT											X	X	
SAT												X	X
ACT												X	X

Checkpoint for Comprehensive Assessment Plan

1. How does an assessment plan help answer the questions related to how we know students have learned what they should be learning?

2. What are the important elements in an assessment plan, and why is such a plan important?

3. Why are both local and state assessments important elements of an assessment plan?

4. What are critical considerations regarding timing and frequency of assessments?

5. How do assessment data contribute to effective curriculum design and implementation?

Scope and Sequence Development

Defining the scope and sequence for learning is the foundational step in the actual curriculum development process. The scope and sequence guides the selection of instructional materials and the development of district assessments. The scope and sequence provide the basis from which specific curriculum guide pages are written to assist teachers in the instruction related to each curricular objective.

1. *What is scope and sequence?* The scope of curriculum is a clearly stated set of K-12 learning objectives that reflects local, state, and national expectations. The sequence is the order in which those objectives are taught. In initial planning, the sequence is established across grades or courses. Later in the process, the order in which objectives are taught at a particular grade level or course is determined; this may take the form of a pacing guide.

2. *Why are scope and sequence important?* The scope-and-sequence document provides the foundation from which a district's curriculum is written. A well articulated scope-and-sequence document provides a clear map of the learning path for students. It also gives teachers a clear picture of the learning that most students coming into their classes will have mastered and helps teachers avoid unconscious duplication of material already learned.

3. *Who develops a district's scope and sequence?* Ideally, the scope and sequence for a curriculum are developed by a curriculum development team who also become the writers of the curriculum guides. The team needs a strong leader and a representative group of teachers committed to the process.

   A. The leader can be a curriculum director, a subject-area specialist, a media specialist, or a principal. The job title of the individual is not important; however, it is important that the leader be committed to the task and have the necessary authority to hold team members accountable for the work they do. If expertise in these skill areas does not exist in the district or if time constraints are a barrier, outside consultant help can be utilized, or teaming with a neighboring district can blend talent pools for common purposes and tasks.

B. The size of the teacher team is dependent on the size of the district, but taking care to not create too large a committee makes for more efficient and effective drafting work. One person per grade level is desirable, but that may stretch small districts. More than one person per grade level creates a large team that may make overall management more difficult. Considerations in putting the team together include the following:

- Expertise in the content area;
- Representation across grade levels; and
- Representation across buildings or areas of the district. If districts blend talents and develop a shared approach, equal or comparable participation needs to be ensured.

C. Once the team is selected, members are trained in the steps needed to develop a sound scope-and-sequence document. Staff development in the writing of curriculum and in developing articulation from level to level within the curriculum design is important. A critical training component is the development of skills to design curriculum that aligns with content, context, and cognitive requirements of state standards and assessments.

Although a relatively small team is involved in the work of developing the scope and sequence and subsequent curriculum documents, review by all teachers who will teach the curriculum and staff, such as media specialists who will support that teaching, is essential. This review includes all grade levels at elementary school and content area teachers at middle and high school levels. A specific process for receiving and evaluating input from the large group of teachers needs to be in place.

4. *When is a scope-and-sequence document developed?* The creation of the scope and sequence is the first step of the curriculum development process. It is also the most critical step as the whole curriculum rests on this foundation. The time span needed to complete the work depends on when the work is being performed and whether there is a current curriculum that allows for revision instead of comprehensive rewriting. The following are possible scenarios for scheduling the work.

- Summer development—with stipends recommended according to district contracts or practices: This can be done in one to two weeks. Input from the writing team in the morning can be word-processed and edited in the afternoon; this work is then reviewed the following morning and serves as the starting point for the next day's work. A scope and sequence produced in this fashion still needs to be presented to the entire faculty at the beginning of the new school year. The process for instructional materials selection can begin after faculty have had input on revisions.

- School year—after school or Saturday work meetings with stipends suggested for this scenario also: A minimum of six meetings is needed, with work from each meeting compiled and edited between meetings and distributed for review prior to the next meeting. If work is spread out over several weeks or months, more time is needed at each meeting to "get back to speed" on the process and remember where previous work had ended. This process begun early in the year provides time for products of the curriculum development team to be circulated among faculty for input and necessary revisions.

- School year—during the school day with substitutes provided: As with other models, the leader and clerical helper need to compile work done at any one session to use as a starting place for the next session. This scenario, when begun early in the year, also provides time for the work of the curriculum development team to be circulated among faculty for input and necessary revisions.

5. ***How does the development of a scope and sequence actually take place?*** The actual process is complex and will be delineated more fully in the "How to" section of this book. The steps below provide a "big picture" of the process.

- Collect materials needed for training.
- Train selected team members.
- Create a backloaded (see Glossary) scope and sequence based on state standards or frameworks and assessments.
- Add objectives determined by local needs.
- Identify and highlight essential learnings to be assessed in district tests (and other measures) and those expected to be tested in other high-stakes assessments.
- Review and edit the draft document.
- Submit the draft of the scope and sequence to stakeholders for review.

- Review and consider all suggestions; make changes as appropriate.
- Finalize scope and sequence.
- Present to district administration for approval, then to the school board.

Checkpoint for Scope and Sequence

1. What is meant by "scope" and by "sequence," and why are they important to curriculum development?

2. When is a scope-and-sequence document best developed, and how is it used?

3. How does a scope-and-sequence document assist teachers and principals?

4. What might be the implications if no scope or sequence has been developed in a curricular area?

Curriculum Guides

Having common educational goals and objectives within a school district brings focus to the work of classroom teachers. Developing documents to guide the instruction in all curricula offered by a school district is critical to effective educational programs and equitable access by all students to the intended curriculum at each grade level and school. The development of a scope-and-sequence document for each curricular area and course is the starting point or foundation for writing curriculum guides. However, quality curriculum guides contain much more than the scope-and-sequence information.

1. *What is a quality curriculum guide?* While the formats of curriculum guides might vary based on local preferences, there are several key elements that contribute significantly to the quality and usefulness of curriculum guides:

   - state and local standards, where applicable, from which curriculum is derived;

- clear learning goals and objectives linked to each standard, stating what students are expected to know and do, how the objective is performed, and the estimated typical time for learning;
- information keying each curriculum objective to district or state performance assessments;
- specific information about prerequisite skills or courses, concepts required before this learning objective (e.g., scope and sequence across grade levels and courses);
- information regarding the primary and supplemental instructional materials to be used, with matches between each objective and the materials provided; and
- specific examples of how key concepts and skills can be approached in the classroom.

2. ***Why is a curriculum guide important for each course offering?*** Without common direction and learning objectives, teachers may unintentionally deliver several different versions of the same courses. Such variations in instructional content leave students at the mercy of chance to achieve equal educational opportunities in the classroom. Likewise, they are left with differing opportunities to learn what is necessary for them to demonstrate knowledge and skills on district or state assessments. The use of curriculum guides is especially helpful for teachers new to the school district and for media specialists and other certified staff who support classroom instruction.

3. ***Who leads/coordinates the development and writing of curriculum guides?*** As described in the previous section regarding the development of a scope-and-sequence, the work is typically accomplished by a team led by a strong leader and involving a representative group of certified personnel, including teachers and media specialists. However, without strong curriculum leadership resources on the staff, districts might choose to contract with a curriculum consultant to lead or coach the project implementation. The writing of curriculum guides is best carried out by the team that designed the scope and sequence because their mastery of the content and contextual rationale for the scope and sequence is likely to be strong. However, some districts choose to expand the working group to include additional staff members on writing teams after the scope-and-sequence document has been completed. In that case, some additional training in the writing of curriculum guides is required to ensure that all participants have the

necessary skills to perform the work. All staff from all grade levels who teach the specific curriculum are involved eventually in reviewing draft guides and providing feedback.

4. ***When are curriculum guides written and revised?*** The cycle of curriculum work is outlined in the table included in the section entitled An Overview of Curriculum Management Planning. The cycle provides a systematic approach to review curriculum and write or revise guides. If no guides are currently present, the content areas for immediate attention are best prioritized to address first those assessed on high-stakes tests at the state and district levels. Another consideration for timing is to address first the curricular areas in which data show low student performance. Further, when state standards or assessments are changed, the local written curriculum needs review and revision as appropriate to align with those changes.

5. ***How are the curriculum guides developed?*** Ideally, several components of the development are in place as part of a curriculum management system for the district and before guide design and development occur. Those components are broadly summarized here and elaborated upon with more details in Section II, Nuts and Bolts:

   - Identify the elements in a curriculum guide that will help teachers and other certified staff, such as librarians, meet the intent of common learning experiences for students (see #1). Develop, or obtain from other sources, different layouts of guide pages to find the one that seems most user-friendly for the staff and provides space for the elements identified.
   - Make sure that the selected format is usable in all curricular areas, not just the area currently being developed. Common formats enhance usefulness by allowing teachers to focus on the content rather than learning new formats.
   - Be sure the guide adequately matches state expectations for content and supportive information where such information is available.
   - Decide whether the guides are to be produced as hard-copy documents, online resources, or both. Even with the current emphasis on using technology, many teachers still prefer to have hard-copy documents at their disposal.
   - Determine the desired format for all curriculum guides based on the considerations of the bullets above. Format of hard-copy

documents and online documents should be as similar as possible for ease of use by teachers. Hot links in electronic documents may appear in hard-copy documents but will be of no help in the paper copies.

Before curriculum guide development work is to begin, the broad clusters of actions necessary are:

- establish a timeline for the development, review, and approval of the curriculum guides. Include timeframes for drafting, review and feedback, board approval, production, distribution, and training in use of the guides and instructional materials adopted with the curriculum;
- select a curriculum development team and identify the leader;
- provide staff development as needed;
- gather informational resources to be used;
- develop the scope-and-sequence document;
- write the curriculum guides;
- conduct review and feedback; modify as needed;
- and complete the process within the timeline, and begin staff development and implementation.

Thoughtfully outlined steps usually result in guides that respond to teacher needs and focus on learning objectives that will be the foundation for aligning the written, taught, and tested curricula. Through this effort, students will then have improved access to the intended common curriculum and a better chance of demonstrating what they know and are able to do in pursuit of state standards and local goals.

Checkpoint for Curriculum Guides

1. Describe the critical contents of a quality curriculum guide.

2. Why is it important to have written curriculum guides for all subjects taught?

3. When and how are guides best developed?

4. Specify the critical steps in designing and writing curriculum guides.

Instructional Materials Selection Process

A critical step to support implementation of an aligned curriculum is the selection of instructional materials to support the subject-area goals and objectives. Efforts to identify the clear and deep alignment of instructional materials with the curriculum will enhance the likelihood of teachers implementing that curriculum in the classroom. (See Glossary and material evaluation forms in Section III.) In states where there are either state-mandated adoptions or a state-selected list of adoptions from which districts are to choose their instructional materials, some "sorting of the alternatives" has already occurred at the state level relative to textbooks as the primary instructional materials. Attention should also be given to the alignment of supplemental instructional materials available both in the classroom and in the media center, but the major focus in the discussion that follows is on textbook adoption.

1. ***What is an instructional materials selection process?*** This process includes review, evaluation, selection, piloting, and adoption of instructional materials to support implementation of the district's curriculum. It includes elements such as:

   • assigned leadership and participation,
   • calendar coordinated with the curriculum development cycle and committee work,
   • vendor/publisher solicitation procedures,
   • guidelines for publisher meetings,
   • designated review steps, and
   • procedures for final adoption of materials.

   A materials selection team collects materials and examines them against the written curriculum using pre-established evaluation forms and developing data summaries of the review. Materials identified as aligning best with the goals and objectives, as well as the intended methodology, are put through a final review. If piloting is part of the process design, the materials tentatively selected from among those given top ratings are piloted before final selections are made and board approval is requested. The piloting process often includes use of materials with the new curriculum in a designated number of classrooms at specified grade levels. Ordering the materials and planning for distribution are the final steps of the process.

2. ***Why is a materials selection process important?*** A process is needed to ensure focus on the appropriateness of various materials for the specific district's curriculum, unless there are single-option, state-mandated textbooks, in which case little local choice will be present. A clear selection process also ensures a fair and thorough review of materials for all affected grade levels, similar treatment of vendors, and professional excellence in evaluating the materials themselves. If timed well, the process can result in materials available for piloted use, for inclusion with specific reference in curriculum guides, and for teachers' guidance as they begin to prepare implementation of the curriculum.

3. ***Who participates in the materials selection process?*** Typically either a district office curriculum staff person, a principal, or a member of the curriculum development team serves as the coordinator/leader of the materials selection process. Having two or three members from the curriculum development team on the selection team is helpful. A library media specialist is a valuable support in locating vendors and resources and in developing a selection policy. Further, the review usually includes involvement of representative school principals, librarians, and teachers from various grades levels. Parents are often invited to participate at some stage of the review, and at least a sample of teachers in the curricular area are involved in piloting materials before final selection.

4. ***When does materials selection occur?*** Several actions are typically either under way or completed before materials selection begins. The learning goals and objectives have been established in a scope-and-sequence document. The instructional philosophy and expected instructional approaches have been delineated. An evaluation form for use in selecting materials is then designed to incorporate criteria related to the goals, objectives, and instructional approaches and appropriate rubrics for rating the materials reviewed. The evaluation form also includes additional factors such as readability and absence of culture and gender biases.

   At this point, sample materials can be solicited from vendors/publishers and prepared for review. Any review of materials prior to completion of the scope-and-sequence document, establishment of clear instructional expectations, and preparation of the materials evaluation forms could result in choices of less aligned materials based on less objective and less focused evaluations. The materials evaluation data are compiled in a user-friendly summary for use in both preliminary and final decisions. Drafts of district assessments are sometimes revised later as materials are selected and guides modified.

It is critical that instructional materials demonstrate clear and deep alignment with the intended learning, including the instructional methodology to be eventually included in the curriculum guide information, and with the assessments to be used. For example, materials to support a specific laboratory class might look quite different from those preferred for a class with integrated curriculum and seminar structure. If such documents as state assessment handbooks or released test items are available, those are considered in the evaluation of materials as well.

Materials are best chosen in time for specific references to be entered into the written curriculum guides. The selection process also occurs far enough in advance of final adoption of the guides so that piloting can include both guides and the tentatively selected materials.

5. ***How is the materials selection process designed?*** To promote clear communication and understanding of the importance of the process, the broad requirements are spelled out in board policy as part of a curriculum management (design/development and delivery) policy. Administrative guidelines or procedures are then developed to spell out the steps and provide specific direction for the work.

Checkpoint for Instructional Materials Selection

1. Describe a typical curriculum materials selection process and how it integrates with curriculum development.

2. What is the alignment evaluation process, and why is it important?

3. When are materials best selected?

Assessment Design and Development

A district-wide comprehensive assessment plan is the starting place for a meaningful assessment program within any school system. That plan (as described earlier) encompasses external and internal assessments, the use of data from those assessments, staff development related to creation, and use of assessments and the data generated from them. The plan provides the foundation for design of assessments related to each curricular area. Understanding of the fundamentals of assessment design is necessary for the development of valid and reliable content-area assessments.

Content-area assessment includes a wide range of methods for ascertaining whether or not students have mastered the desired knowledge and skills. Assessments may be summative—at the classroom, school, or district level—or formative. Formative assessment occurs at the classroom level; it enables teachers to make timely decisions about adjusting instruction for the whole group or for individual students. Multiple kinds of assessments covering the same content reduce reliance on a single assessment for determining whether or not students have mastered the content.

1. ***What is involved in assessment design?*** In his book *Student-Centered Classroom Assessment*, Rick Stiggins lists the following considerations that are critical to high-quality assessment design:

   - clearly defined expectations for student learning,
   - the purpose for any assessment,
   - the assessment methods (such as multiple choice or performance, machine scored versus teacher graded),
   - the sampling of the content that will be included versus all the content that could be included, and
   - elimination of bias that might distort results (14-17).

   Attention to these considerations will help ensure development of assessments that provide valid and reliable information about student achievement.

2. ***Why is assessment design important?*** Each of the five considerations listed above has a different implication for the importance of assessment design.

   - Too often questions that students are asked to respond to on a test do not match the specified learning objectives for a course. This occurs especially when tests that accompany commercial materials, used in many states across the nation, are used to measure learning related to the curricular standards in a specific state.
   - A test that provides a benchmark for student achievement across a district will not be the same as a teacher-made assessment that diagnoses whether or not students—collectively or individually—are ready to move on to the next concept.

- The method for assessment is frequently determined by the purpose for assessment. Determining whether or not students have mastered basic skills or concepts might call for a short-answer or multiple-choice test. A performance task may be a better means of assessing a student's ability to apply a range of cumulative or connected knowledge.

- It would be very difficult, if not impossible, to assess—either formally or informally—all the content that students are expected to learn. Decisions are made about a representative sample of concepts and skills to be included on any given assessment.

- Deep alignment between local assessments of curriculum objectives and state assessments in use should focus on providing a range of assessment methods that will allow students to learn and experience different ways to demonstrate their knowledge or skills so that whatever types of assessment items are in use, they can respond knowledgeably. Application of current brain research information can contribute significantly to the development of effective, meaningful assessments at the local level.

- Elimination of bias does not refer only to ethnicity or gender. Reading difficulty or length of tests are just two areas, which, if not carefully considered in assessment design, could distort information gleaned from assessments. Occasionally, contextual references are included that have not yet been part of the students' experience socially, intellectually, or geographically.

In addition to these considerations, test writers should also consider the context and cognitive type of individual items on external assessments and include items with similar context and cognition demands on local assessments. Attention to these factors will enable students to transfer more readily the knowledge and skills assessed on both sets of tests. This match between local and external assessments is one aspect of deep alignment.

3. ***Who develops assessments used within a school system?*** Responsibility of assessment development within a district rests upon individuals at different levels within the organization.

- Development of criterion-referenced tests that will be used across the district is the responsibility of a district-level administrator. That individual will choose a small but representative team that includes teachers at various levels to oversee development of tests.

- Diagnostic tests that teachers use to determine students' preknowledge and mastery of a given objective can be developed either at the district level, by grade-level or department teams, or by individual teachers.
- Formative and summative assessments (see Glossary) used by individual classroom teachers are developed by those teachers.

In all cases, individuals involved in creating assessments need a sound foundation in assessment design that comes through appropriate staff development.

If expertise does not exist within the district for development of district-wide assessments, or if multiple responsibilities limit the time available for test development, services of outside consultants can be utilized to develop desired assessments.

4. ***When are content-area assessments developed?*** It is desirable that the creation of the district-wide assessment plan precede any work on content-area assessments. However, with or without a district-wide assessment plan, creation of district assessments in a given content area can begin once the scope-and-sequence document is finalized.

Classroom teachers develop both formative and summative assessments during the implementation of a newly revised curriculum. A clearly defined set of learning objectives for each course, based on the scope and sequence, is the prerequisite for developing assessments of any type.

5. ***How are assessments in a given content area developed?*** The following considerations will lead to the development of sound district-wide assessments. More specific details on each of these considerations are included in Section II of this book.

- Develop a content-area assessment plan for each grade level at the elementary school or each course at the secondary level. This plan will include the type and number of assessments, how the assessments will be administered, and how they will be scored. The content-area plan fits under the umbrella of the district's assessment plan and is consistent with that plan in all aspects.
- Review the results of required internal and external assessments to help determine areas of local assessment emphasis.

- Incorporate information about the types of assessment items, how students are expected to respond, and with what given information when designing the content area assessments.
- Determine the content objectives that will be included on each assessment, and then select or write items that specifically measure those objectives.
- Have a pre-established process for reviewing the content of assessments for validity and reliability and then revising the assessments as necessary.

Attention to several areas will assist classroom teachers in creating a variety of formative and summative assessments that will provide usable data to guide instructional and programmatic decision-making. These areas include staff development in appropriate use of different kinds of assessment, training in writing test items that match specific learning objectives from the district's adopted curriculum, and time for teachers to work collaboratively to develop common assessments and review assessment results.

Checkpoint for Assessment Design and Development

1. What factors are considered in designing assessments?

2. Why is it important to do the assessment design well?

Staff Development and Curriculum Implementation

With scope and sequence, curriculum guides, materials selection, and assessments completed, the next step includes staff development and curriculum implementation.

1. *What is involved in staff development and curriculum implementation?* Staff development focused on the new curriculum and materials is the foundation for successful implementation of a new or revised curriculum. The staff development is designed for teachers and administrators prior to use of the new curriculum and instructional materials in the classrooms. Ideally, some staff development also

continues during curriculum implementation to address emerging needs with use of the new curriculum or instructional materials.

This stage also includes communication with parents and other community members regarding the changes involved. This communication might include parent newsletters, informational events, and grade-level curriculum brochures.

2. *Why is it necessary to plan implementation?* Unless carefully planned steps are taken to ensure readiness for curriculum implementation, confusion and other problems can easily surface among the teachers or with parents and community members. These two constituencies need to be well informed about the changes that have been adopted, and teachers particularly need to have support in developing comfort and confidence as implementation begins. Without support, the tendency among staff can be to "fall back" on comforts of curriculum content and instructional materials. Parents and community members develop confidence in what is occurring when they are well informed with specific written information for ongoing reference. It is important not to leave implementation preparation to chance if these needs are to be met effectively.

3. *Who is involved in implementation steps?* A staff member is designated to coordinate the planning of staff development for the curriculum "orientation," preferably with team leaders from the curriculum development phase conducting the training. Often grade-level leaders from elementary schools or department chairs at the secondary level assume leadership for the staff development; in other instances, individuals with expertise in the new curriculum are the trainers. Librarians are helpful when curriculum materials are online or when use of library resources is an integral part of the new curriculum. To provide information to parents and the community, designated curriculum committee members and other staff members can prepare the informational brochures by grade level for elementary curriculum and by course for secondary.

4. *When does implementation begin?* Once the curriculum guides and instructional materials are prepared, the staff development for implementation can begin. Certainly at least part of the training occurs prior to teachers being required to use the curriculum and materials in their classrooms. A staff development component easily ignored is the availability of annual training for teachers and other certified

staff, such as librarians new to the school district, after the initial orientation sessions. The parent and community informational materials are prepared immediately and disseminated as soon as possible either before or during the initial stage of implementation.

5. ***How is curriculum implementation planned and carried out?*** A plan for both the staff development and communication steps during implementation is carefully planned in advance. These two steps, including ongoing follow-up training sessions, are scheduled and the calendar shared with teachers to assure them that there is some continuing support. The new curriculum and related materials are made available as soon as possible to all teachers expected to use them. They need the opportunity to become familiar with them in a general way at first. Subsequently, they receive training in specific content of the curriculum and the correlating materials, including how the curriculum and materials align with the state standards and assessments to be used. In some instances, grade-level teams and department chairs coordinate follow-up sessions, and the teachers conduct their own ongoing development with members of the curriculum development team(s) assisting.

The implementation plan must include training for teachers who will use the new curriculum and materials, the principals who will supervise the implementation, specialty teachers such as librarians who will support the curriculum, and parents. The training is designed specifically for each group, based on the particular job duties of people within the group. Many districts provide training for certified staff, such as teachers and librarians, who work directly with students, while few design training for principals and parents. Training for these groups is a critical component for program success.

Brochures that explain the new curriculum can be given to parents by teachers, either at back-to-school events or through some other kind of personal contact. Brochures should also be readily available in the principal's office in every school and at the district office. Another popular approach for parents is to hold curriculum "fairs" or "forums" at which the new information is made available to them. An effective preparation step is to inform parents in school newsletters and the general public in the local newspaper that changes are occurring and that written information is available upon request. This information can also be posted on the Web page of a school or a school's library, as well as the district's Web page. Parents may be more apt to read information posted by the school their children attend.

Along with staff development and communication steps, monitoring and supervision of curriculum development is a significant component of implementation. (See Section I, Monitoring Curriculum Delivery.)

Checkpoint for Staff Development

1. Why is staff development important to curriculum design and implementation?

2. What are some important considerations in planning and designing staff development for curriculum implementation?

3. How should staff development and the plans for curriculum implementation be integrated?

Monitoring Curriculum Delivery

With a curriculum in place and staff development on implementation of the curriculum and use of accompanying instructional materials under way, teachers are now ready to translate the curriculum into classroom instruction. There will be a continuing need for support and guidance, not just ongoing training, but also coaching and conversations about the curriculum and its implementation. This is the stage referred to as "monitoring," but it does not refer only to supervision. This phase can include a range of activities that benefit teachers and students and enhance the school district's chance of attaining its educational goals. Monitoring activities then inform both program evaluation and curriculum revision.

1. *What is monitoring?* Monitoring includes the various activities undertaken by district and school administrators and by teacher teams to observe curriculum implementation. It fulfills several purposes:

   • identify barriers to student mastery of the objectives,
   • discuss any strengths or problems with the related materials, and
   • clarify instructional successes and problems related to the curriculum.

Typically, classroom visits by district and school administrators, review of lesson plans, exchange visits among teachers, and grade-level or departmental dialogue are components of the planned monitoring of curriculum implementation. Regardless of the specific activities, conversation and feedback are critical elements of effective monitoring.

2. ***Why is curriculum monitoring important?*** Without a systematic approach to monitoring of curriculum implementation, it is difficult to identify related needs of teachers and students and to intervene to make implementation effective. Additionally, sound and varied monitoring practices ensure that the adopted curriculum is being taught by all teachers so that all students have equal access to the curriculum. Monitoring activities also assist in identification of problems or issues for consideration during the program evaluation phase of curriculum work. Many teaching staffs (including grade-level teams or department teams) have found that monitoring activities help preclude misunderstandings and confusion about curriculum changes.

3. ***Who is responsible for curriculum monitoring?*** Curriculum monitoring is a shared responsibility. Central office administrators and staff working in the areas of curriculum design and staff development need to be included in part of the monitoring activities, especially school/classroom visits and occasional staff dialogues. The key leaders and participants for curriculum monitoring, however, are the school principals (and assistant principals, where applicable). Teachers themselves can also be significant participants in curriculum monitoring. As a part of ongoing monitoring, teachers are often encouraged to share the work of designing model lesson plans, developing new activities to support the curriculum changes, and integrating curriculum across subject areas.

4. ***When does curriculum monitoring occur?*** Ideally curriculum monitoring begins soon after the staff development orientation to curriculum and instructional materials as teachers begin using the new curriculum in classroom instruction. Monitoring is introduced during staff development and staff meetings as one of the instructional support activities as well as a curriculum supervision practice. Frequent observations, conversations, and progress checks then become ongoing components of the monitoring function. When principals and assistant principals have experienced the staff

development related to curriculum with their teachers, the monitoring function has a greater relevance to both administrator and teacher roles and to the collaboration desired during implementation.

5. *How is curriculum monitoring carried out?* A variety of monitoring activities have been successful in different schools across the states. It is helpful if the district and school administrators establish a "protocol" or set of expectations regarding curriculum monitoring and communicate that information to all certified staff. Additionally, teachers can be invited to offer suggestions for monitoring practices that they deem helpful.

Usually, the district office administrators (or curriculum staff) coordinate planning and training for curriculum monitoring. They also participate in monitoring by visiting classrooms, either with the principal or independently, and by engaging in staff conversations at school staff, grade-level, or departmental meetings. These are the personnel who obtain a system-wide picture of the curriculum implementation issues and can contribute to program evaluation with that broad-based information. The principals set the tone for collegial development and professional growth through a supportive coaching approach. Frequent classroom visits to identify critical curriculum implementation topics or issues and participation in dialogues with grade-level teams or departmental teams are two of the principals' monitoring activities. Classroom observations by district and building-level administrators and follow-up conversations related to those observations can be made more productive through training such as *The 3-Minute Classroom Walk-through.* Reviewing teachers' lesson plans on a regular basis or having teachers keep track of curriculum implementation in a systematic way are practical steps to help school administrators get a picture of implementation progress by individual teachers or by grade level or department.

Classroom visit exchanges, team "debriefings" and conversations, and shared lesson-designing activities can be effective monitoring activities in which teachers participate. Periodic surveys regarding a new or modified curriculum, related materials, or such problems as pacing of learning objectives can also be useful. Information from ongoing monitoring activities feed into program evaluation, curriculum planning, and related curriculum review activities.

Checkpoint for Monitoring Curriculum Delivery

1. What are some ways in which the implementation of curriculum can be monitored?

2. Why is this function more than just a supervisory practice?

3. Who are the parties typically involved in curriculum monitoring?

4. Describe some approaches to effective curriculum monitoring.

Assessment Implementation and Data Use

A successful district-wide assessment program depends upon four key ingredients: an overall assessment plan that guides all assessment and evaluation with the district, well-designed assessments with items that specifically match student learning expectations, ethical and consistent test administration and implementation, and appropriate use of data derived from the assessments. The first two considerations have been addressed in Comprehensive Assessment Plan and Assessment Design and Development. The discussion that follows describes the considerations relevant to district-wide test implementation and use of data; some of the discussion may apply to teacher-made assessments as well.

1. *What is involved in assessment implementation and use of data?*
Procedures related to district-wide assessment administration include attention to security of assessments when deemed necessary, clear and specific instructions for test administration, and adherence to those instructions by individuals administering the assessments.

Use of data includes organization and analysis of data. Appropriate analysis of data requires staff development for all individuals who will use the data. The ultimate use of data occurs in the planning and delivery of instruction, when teachers and librarians make instructional decisions based on the data available to them.

2. *Why are appropriate implementation and use of data important?*
Unless consistent procedures are developed and followed in the administration of tests, results lack validity and reliability. When procedures are followed, and when there is confidence that data are valid and reliable, those results provide the basis for meaningful action steps based on the data. Data are not collected just for the sake of having data; assessment results guide programmatic decision-making at the district and building level and instructional decision-making at the classroom level.

3. ***Who is responsible for assessment implementation and use of data?***

- Any district employee involved with instruction, curriculum development, and assessment will have some responsibility for assessment administration and use of data.
- District-level assessment personnel have the overall responsibility for test production, preparation of appropriate instructions for administration, test dissemination, provisions for scoring, and training in data interpretation.
- District-level curriculum personnel will use the data in program evaluation and as a basis for revision in curriculum development.
- Building administrators will oversee administration of assessments in their respective buildings and will work with classroom teachers to make decisions at both the building and classroom level related to building programs and instructional strategies and modifications.
- Classroom teachers, in most cases, will be responsible for administering assessments according to protocol, interpreting data relative to their own students, and making instructional decisions based on the data.

4. ***When will analysis of data occur, and how soon should interventions take place?*** One of the most important aspects of any assessment program is the timely availability of data. In planning for test administration and scoring, quick turnaround is a high priority. Analysis of data occurs just as soon as data are available. Appropriate teacher interventions in the classroom follow data analysis. There is often a complexity of multiple issues within the school units or district that impact the time required to access aggregated and disaggregated data. However, it is critical that the data dissemination and analysis take place within a reasonable timeframe in order to impact teacher planning to meet student needs.

5. ***How can district personnel become proficient in appropriate use of data?*** Appropriate use of data begins with staff development. Training issues have been discussed under Comprehensive Assessment Plan and Assessment Design and Development. Understanding and application of assessment vocabulary, meaningful organization and presentation of data, and interpretation of data are key components of training relevant to data use. If district personnel at any level— classroom to superintendent and board of education—are to make

appropriate instructional decisions based on the data, then familiarity with district curriculum and the relevance of any assessment to the curriculum is crucial. Data that sit in a file cabinet or on a shelf are of no value for the district, the staff, or the students.

Checkpoint for Assessment Implementation and Data Use

1. What is involved in implementation of assessment?

2. What is included in "data use?"

3. Who are the persons most likely to use data, and how are their various uses similar and different?

4. What should be the critical impacts of appropriate data use?

Program Evaluation

The list of programs in place in almost any school system is a lengthy one. A typical list includes curriculum for core content areas and electives, extra- and co-curricular programs, ancillary programs related to both content and personal skills, motivational programs, discipline program . . . the list could go on and on. The commercial providers of many materials promote their product as the answer to a multitude of problems. District personnel develop and implement curriculum that is intended to enable students to be successful in learning required knowledge and skills. The truth of the matter is that some programs work while others do not. Some programs need to be discarded while others have a powerful influence and support district goals for student learning. It is through program evaluation that the value of programs can be determined.

1. *What is program evaluation?* Program evaluation is the systematic review of programs in place in a district or programs that are being considered for implementation. The evaluation process collects qualitative and quantitative data related to the effectiveness of these programs in order to make determinations about adopting, maintaining, eliminating, or modifying them.

2. ***Why is program evaluation important?*** The purpose for programs within a district is to either directly impact teaching and learning or support those activities. The education of children is too important and resources are too limited to spend time and money implementing programs that do not have a positive impact on learning. It is imperative that those programs which are essential to students' success in life be of highest possible quality, while those programs that are not contributing to success be eliminated. Program evaluation is the process that enables these conditions and decisions. Program evaluation can facilitate identification of misalignment between programs and district goals.

3. ***Who is responsible for program evaluation?*** The board of education sets the expectation for program evaluation through board policy. The development of a process for program evaluation is the responsibility of central office administration. Implementation of program evaluation may fall upon different district personnel, depending on the program being evaluated. Input from parents and community members can be solicited as part of the process.

4. ***When does program evaluation occur?*** There are two times when program evaluation is most appropriate. The first time occurs before a new program is purchased or implemented, includes careful reviews of the program, and determines the probability that the program will meet the needs of the district or the problem it is intended to solve. This evaluation is similar to (but not identical to) the needs assessment in the curriculum development cycle. The second time when program evaluation is appropriate is after the implementation of a new program or curriculum. It is evaluation at this point that is the focus of the stage described here. A plan for evaluation is established before the program is implemented in the classroom. Formal evaluation of the efficacy of a revised curriculum occurs after the program has had at least one full year of implementation.

5. ***How is program evaluation carried out?*** A formal plan for evaluation is established before the rollout of the new or revised curriculum. Specific and measurable goals are set, using baseline data from the year before implementation where appropriate. The needs assessment may provide some of the baseline information. Interviews and surveys can be a source of both quantitative and qualitative data. Personnel responsible for the evaluation are identified, with their specific tasks

delineated. A timeline for the entire process is established. Procedures for follow-up activities, based on results of the evaluation, are included in the plan.

Checkpoint for Program Evaluation

1. What is meant by program evaluation, and why is it important?

2. What factors should be considered in program evaluation, and what information contributes to this function?

3. How does student assessment data support quality program evaluation?

4. How is program evaluation carried out?

5. How does program evaluation fit into the work of curriculum design and development?

Section II • Nuts and Bolts

Introduction: "How To" Steps

As noted in Section I, curriculum management planning is a comprehensive function intended to produce a system for effective design, development, implementation, and evaluation of a district's curriculum. The planning includes several stages of work and should be established and communicated in a comprehensive curriculum management policy with administrative procedures or a board-adopted plan to direct the processes.

The "how to" chapters in Section II present detailed actions necessary to carry out that function in steps consistent with the overview of curriculum management planning in Section I. The basic elements of this planning function include the following items.

- ✔ A needs assessment
- ✔ A curriculum development/review cycle
- ✔ An assessment plan that incorporates state and district assessments of student learning correlated with state expectations and district curriculum
- ✔ Scope-and-sequence documents for curriculum areas
- ✔ Curriculum guides for teachers in all curriculum areas, including librarians and media specialists
- ✔ Instructional materials selection
- ✔ Design and development of assessments for curriculum
- ✔ Staff development to support stages of design, delivery, and evaluation of the curriculum, including effective use of data
- ✔ Curriculum monitoring processes for administrators and teachers
- ✔ Assessment implementation and data use
- ✔ Program evaluation for decision-making

Section II address each of these elements of curriculum management planning.

How To: Needs Assessment

In needs assessment, the focus is on identification of strengths, weaknesses, or problems within the educational program before designing initiatives or launching changes in curriculum. A well-crafted needs assessment will generate information about gaps in programs and curriculum, unsatisfactory results from current efforts, anticipated changes in the district and state expectations for students, and unmet needs of students as reflected in current data.

Conducting the needs assessment involves specific steps:

1. Establish leadership for the needs assessment. A leader can come from within the organization if skills and experience exist in areas of issue identification, question design, and data compilation and analysis. Without this expertise, district leaders can contract for external process leadership for the assessment and data analysis.

2. Select a needs assessment team. The designated leader should choose a team small enough to function efficiently and large enough to have adequate representation of appropriate stakeholders. Typically these teams are comprised of seven to 10 people. Teams can include persons from various levels of the organization who are knowledgeable about the development and use of data, critical thinkers who can see the "big picture" and how the parts fit into the whole, and those who can clearly articulate questions and issues. Members should also have demonstrated skills in analyzing and applying data to decision-making. A library media specialist can provide invaluable support as part of the team in providing research support and identifying available materials.

3. Clarify the questions to be answered during needs assessment. The team clarifies and documents the specific questions in order to focus the selection of data that will be included in the needs assessment. Input from teachers within the system is helpful in this area. Figure 3.1 in Section III provides a sample survey, while Figure 3.2 provides results from an actual survey.

4. Determine what information is currently available. The team should identify potentially useful information from such sources as:

   • written statements of district vision, goals, or outcomes for the educational program;

- federal expectations and state standards or curriculum;
- information about future expectations from federal and state sources;
- current research articles and resources;
- current written district curriculum;
- school-based and district disaggregated test data (past three to five years); and
- constituent survey responses.

Figure 3.3 in Section III provides a sample list of data sources to be considered.

5. Identify what information is missing and how to obtain it. E.g., if no survey data are available, how will that feedback information be acquired?

   - By external assistance,
   - by brief school-based staff and parent/student surveys, or
   - by accessing state or county data sources?

   Or, if no test data reports are available by ethnicity or socio-economic factors, how can the team obtain that level of information disaggregated by the school and district?

6. Prioritize the data collection tasks. This step includes matching the data to the questions and reviewing what the group determined in Step 5 to be sure team members spend time wisely and find the desired answers.

7. Access curriculum research information. The group reviews studies and reports from current curriculum research to identify additional information that might be necessary or beneficial to the decisions.

8. Identify clearly stated performance standards and expectations against which the current conditions or status can be compared. The team should include both external (such as federal and state) and internal

(community and school district) statements of expectations, goals, or standards. Certainly include the indicators of Annual Yearly Progress (AYP).

9. Assign study and analysis tasks to complete the assessment work. Using the data compiled and the criteria and questions identified, analyze the data and summarize the findings.

10. Decide upon a data report format and compile the report. After compiling the data (Steps 4 through 7 on pages 42–43), the team determines the appropriate format for data display and a format for the entire needs assessment report. Minimum contents should be:

   • introduction (the who, what, when, why, and how of the needs assessment—including standards and expectations as well as methods of analysis used in the needs assessment);
   • executive summary of "findings" or results of the needs assessment (the key points derived from the data analysis);
   • detailed discussion of questions included in the assessment and the needs identified through the assessment data (including tables and charts where applicable to simplify display of data); and
   • related documents (timetable, sources of responses, research sources).

11. Disseminate the needs assessment report. The team should provide the report to all persons within the organization who are involved in educational program and operational decision-making. Team members should be available to hear feedback and discuss with respondents.

12. Revise report as needed in response to feedback.

13. Establish ongoing resource support to users of the assessment report. Team members should be available as resources to the decision-makers at district and school levels who will use the needs assessment report to review curriculum, related educational programs, student assessment design, and specific organizational operations and functions. The completed needs assessment can be used as a source of baseline data during curriculum development and revision work and when program evaluation is conducted some time after curriculum implementation.

How To: Curriculum Development Cycle

A curriculum development cycle is a systematic schedule or calendar for addressing the design, delivery, and review of curriculum in all content areas. The components of the cycle include needs assessment, curriculum development or revision, materials selection, assessment development, curriculum implementation—including staff development, and program evaluation for each content area. Planning for curriculum development within a cycle allows district personnel to address ongoing curricular and instructional needs in a timely manner.

1. Determine district personnel who will establish the cycle. These individuals should have knowledge of and responsibility for budget, resources, and curriculum.

2. Establish the time period that the curriculum cycle will encompass. The period should be long enough to include all core and elective subjects. A typical cycle for a given content area may cover a five- to seven-year span. In some states, a cycle might be determined by a state-mandated process for selecting new textbooks in a particular content area.

Initial development of the cycle will be influenced by several factors. These include existing state cycles for revision or textbooks adoption, national standards revision, available financial resources, student assessment performance, and capacity of district personnel to do the work.

The table in Figure 2.1 (also shown in Section I) is one example of a cycle that would cover the four core content areas.

Figure 2.1
A Sample Curriculum Development Cycle

	Needs Assessment	Curriculum Development	Materials Selection	Implementation	Program Evaluation
Math	Year 1	Year 2	Year 2	Year 3	Year 5
Lang. Arts	Year 2	Year 3	Year 3	Year 4	Year 6
Science	Year 3	Year 4	Year 4	Year 5	Year 7
Soc. St.	Year 4	Year 5	Year 5	Year 6	Year 8

A cycle like the one shown in the table would spread major textbook purchases across time, lessening the impact on budgets. Elementary school teachers who teach all subjects would not be expected to implement more than one new core curriculum in a given year.

Figures 3.4 and 3.5 in Section III provide samples of curriculum review cycles with more detail than the table above, but without reference to specific content areas. Figures 3.6 and 3.7 are examples of cycles with content areas included. Finally, Figure 3.8 is a typical outline for the first year of revision in a given content area.

How To: Comprehensive Assessment Plan Development

As noted in Section I, Comprehensive Assessment Plan, the creation and administration of assessments aligned with the district's curriculum and use of data obtained from those assessments is crucial to the measurement of students' learning and the modification of instruction to increase learning. While many people will be involved with the assessment process—students, classroom teachers, building administrators, and district administrators—the work of all those individuals should be guided by a well-thought out assessment plan that addresses the many kinds of assessment and the needs of various stakeholders.

1. Select a small team of individuals who are knowledgeable about assessment to develop the initial draft of an assessment plan. The team should include the district personnel responsible for assessment, an individual with information technology responsibilities at the district level, and representatives from building administrators. One or two teachers with an interest and expertise in assessment would be good members of the team.

2. Set a timeline for development of the plan. While the timeline may change slightly as you work, you need to set a reasonable timeframe initially so the project will be completed in a timely manner.

3. Determine the components that you will include in your assessment plan. The planning should consider the following:

- **A rationale for testing.** This will include a mission statement and a philosophy of assessment. Why are assessments administered in your district? While current legislation requires you to do so, there are other sound educational reasons that you should consider. Figure 3.9 in Section III provides a sample of a district philosophy.
- **A list of assessments that will be administered.** Assessments range from high-stakes external assessments such as state assessments and College Board exams to district-wide criterion referenced tests. (See Figures 3.9 and 3.10 in Section III.)
- **A district assessment calendar.** District staff, students, and parents all need a big picture of what required assessments will be given and when they will be administered. (See Figure 3.11 in Section III.)
- **Collection, organization, and dissemination of assessment results.** Data arrive in various ways. Sometimes the data are returned from an external source in electronic form or hard copy. Local data may be obtained through technological resources but may also come through paper/pencil methods. Whatever the method for collecting data, questions about communicating results must be answered. How will data be organized for dissemination? Who will get what in the way of results?
- **Staff development.** Ongoing staff development in the use of data is essential if the assessment process is to make a difference in student learning. Training should address many aspects of assessment: the kinds of assessments being used in the district and the purposes for each; interpretation of the data from any assessment; ways to modify instruction based on assessment results; and development of sound local assessments, for both district-wide and individual classroom use.

Technology Tip

Develop your assessment plan from the very beginning with input from those individuals in information technology who will support implementation. A plan is only as good as the infrastructure that supports it.

- **Test protocol and security.** If data are to be collected district-wide, you will need to develop specific protocols for test administration. If you determine that security is necessary for some tests, you need to address the issue of storage (either for hard copies or for electronic copies).

- **Resources.** A district assessment program requires both human and financial resources. Consideration of these should be included in an assessment plan so that funds can be appropriated in the district budgeting process.
- **Assess the assessment plan.** In developing an assessment plan, it would be wise to build in a requirement for periodic review of the plan. You want to be sure that the plan continues to meet the needs of a changing scene—both in your district and by mandates of federal and state legislation.

4. Don't reinvent the wheel. Go to the work of known and respected experts in the assessment field to determine current research-based practices. (Suggestions are included in the Reference section of this book.) Check the Web sites of other districts to find examples of good assessment plans that might guide your thinking.

5. Begin writing the plan, once your team has identified the components of the district's assessment plan and you have researched the topic to your satisfaction. A single individual can do the writing, or it can be assigned to different individuals, but the final product needs to read with one voice. Regardless of who does the writing, the entire team needs to read, review, and make suggestions for change before the document is disseminated any further.

6. Share the plan with a wider audience after the assessment planning team approves the initial draft. The wider audience should include all district staff with assessment and curriculum responsibilities, all building administrators, and any other stakeholders identified by the team.

7. Review and consider the suggestions for change from the larger audience, making appropriate modifications to the final document.

8. Take the finalized draft of the comprehensive assessment plan to the superintendent for approval and then to the school board either as an information item or for approval if district policy requires board approval.

How To: Scope and Sequence Development

As noted in Section I, Scope and Sequence Development, the creation of a scope and sequence is the basis for all subsequent curriculum work in any content area. The scope-and-sequence document is used to establish pacing throughout the year and to guide creation of district-wide assessments and selection of instructional resources. Well-written objectives in the scope-and-sequence document enable the creation of curriculum guides. Curriculum guides, in turn, assist teachers in planning lessons with appropriate instructional strategies and assessments that promote maximum student achievement of each objective. The importance of "getting it right" at this stage cannot be overemphasized!

1. Select the curriculum development team members. The composition of your curriculum team can make or break the process. You need to think about the team leader, the size and structure of your team, and how to select members of the team.

   A. Team leader: As noted in the Overview section on scope and sequence, the leader can be someone from within the district or an external consultant/leader. Choices from district personnel might include a curriculum director, a subject area specialist, or a building-level administrator. The team leader needs some expertise in both the curriculum development process and the content area under consideration. The leader should have the authority to hold team members accountable for the work required to accomplish the task. At the same time, the leader needs to have the interpersonal skills necessary to encourage team members, build consensus, and facilitate the entire process. In other words, be firm, but not heavy-handed.

   B. Size and structure: The number of people on the team will depend somewhat on the size of the district.

      • In mid-sized to large school districts, representation from each grade level, K-8, is desirable, with teachers of required high school courses also included. For example, in English/Language Arts, include a teacher from each grade level (9-12). In mathematics, teachers of Algebra 1, Geometry, and Algebra 2 should be part of the team, with one teacher representative from higher-level mathematics courses. More than one person per grade or course can lead to an unwieldy team; others can be involved in feedback at a later stage. Including a media specialist as a team member will result in expanded knowledge of print and electronic resources by the entire team, especially in content areas where teachers may not be aware of the media options available to them. In smaller districts it may be necessary to function with fewer teachers. In this situation, representatives across levels are needed—primary, intermediate, middle school, and high school.

• Some building administrators may want to be involved in the revision process. If there are principals on the team (other than the team leader), clearly establish the position of those principals as team members—not leaders. The authors have been involved in situations where building administrators who were accustomed to authority within their own buildings wanted to have the same authority on a curriculum team; this situation can impede the entire curriculum development process.

C. Selection of members: Expertise in and enthusiasm for the content area are critical attributes for team members. The selection process will vary, depending on the size of the district.

• In small systems, district or building-level administrators may know exactly who the right people are for a specific revision team. It is important, however, that the same "good people" not be recruited for every revision team. Across time, the involvement of as many people as possible in various content areas leads to far greater faculty buy-in than if the same people are doing the work all the time.

• In larger systems, building-level administrators can recommend teachers from their buildings whom they consider to be good candidates for the curriculum development team or there can be an application process. From a list of recommendations and applications, the team leader and any other administrators concerned with the composition of the team can choose team members that will include individuals from each grade level who also represent schools from various locations within the district.

- Team members will want to know "what they are getting into." Before recruiting a curriculum development team in districts of any size, district leaders should be ready to share an outline of responsibilities and a general timeline for the task. An important decision is whether teachers will be involved only with scope and sequence, or whether some or all will have a broader involvement for curriculum guide development. (The scope and sequence is the critical foundation but only a small part of an entire curriculum guide.)
- Sample recommendation forms for principals, application forms, and letters of invitation to selected teachers are included in Section III if your district chooses to use these types of procedural communication. (See Figure 3.12 in Section III for a sample application form. Typical letters to different stakeholders are included in Figure 3.12 on the CD.)

2. Collect materials needed for training. Good news! The materials needed for training are very similar to those required for the needs assessment, so you will need little extra effort to assemble them. The following documents will provide the direction needed by the personnel working on scope and sequence:

- written statements of the district vision and goals for the educational program;
- data from the needs assessment;
- state standards or curriculum documents for the content area under consideration;
- national standards and current research related to the content area;
- information related to objectives addressed by mandated assessments (state assessments, norm-referenced, college entrance) and performance on those assessments;
- the most recently written curriculum for the content area; and
- access to software that writers will use in creating documents. Identification of the software will be part of the initial planning process.

As noted in How To: Needs Assessment, a district media specialist can provide support in conducting research and finding helpful resources. A checklist is included in Section III to be used in keeping track of data and documents that are available within a district and can be used in both needs assessment and curriculum development work. (See Figure 3.3 in the Needs Assessment division in Section III.) Two examples of additional scope-and-sequence and curriculum-development training documents are found in Figure 3.13.

3. Train selected team members. Regardless of the subject matter, there is basic training in deep curriculum alignment that is applicable for all content areas. Team members need training in:

- the steps required in developing a scope-and-sequence document;
- the foundational principles of curriculum development, as described in the Overview of Curriculum Management Planning;
- how to interpret and use correctly the terminology of curriculum work (alignment, articulation, coordination, standards, goals, objectives, indicators);
- how to identify contextual elements in curriculum goals and objectives and in assessment items;
- how to recognize cognitive domains and types and to use the language of cognition appropriately;
- how to write clear objectives using contextual information and cognitive language;
- how to identify and create deep alignment across the written, taught, and tested curriculum; and
- how to use the software that has been selected for curriculum writing.

Technology Tip

Designate a "Curriculum Development" folder on a district server accessible only to the district's curriculum team. Writers should consistently save their work to that location as well as to auxiliary storage devices such as flash drives.

The understanding of deep alignment is critical for those individuals involved in curriculum development. The research on the impact of deep alignment spans almost a century. In his book, *Deciding What to Teach and Test*, Fenwick English built on the conceptual theories of alignment and transfer developed by Edward Thorndike (85). In the early 1900s Thorndike established the concept of transfer, which is enhanced when contexts for learning, application, and assessment are similar. Brain research from the 1990s has not only reinforced Thorndike's findings, but also has found evidence that the more ways a student is asked to demonstrate knowledge, the deeper that student's understanding of the knowledge. This latter finding is especially important when considering types of assessment.

4. Align the written curriculum with that which is tested. No one has articulated the need for alignment of the written, taught, and tested curriculum better than Fenwick English in both *Deciding What to Teach and Test* and *Deep Curriculum Alignment*. The written curriculum must reflect the knowledge and skills for which students are held accountable on mandated external assessments.

    To achieve the alignment between the written and tested curriculum, create a scope-and-sequence matrix that is based on assessed content on high stakes assessments such as state tests and College Board exams. This is called backloading. To backload, utilize the assessment blueprints provided by your state or any other document that describes the content of the assessment. To determine the format and context of assessments, analyze released items through the process of item deconstruction. Deconstruction involves analyzing the vocabulary used in an item, what is required to demonstrate the knowledge or skill in the item, the prior knowledge that is required, and the format of the item. (See Figure 3.14 for an activity illustrating deconstruction.)

    Curriculum writers use different approaches when writing objectives for each grade level.

    • Some writers choose to include objectives at levels of introduction, mastery, and reinforcement.
    • Others include only objectives that are to be mastered at the grade where the objective appears. Objectives may spiral in difficulty across grades so that an objective at one grade is a prerequisite (a necessary introduction) for a subsequent grade, but mastery is expected of all objectives included at a specific grade. Objectives mastered at one grade level are reinforced through use at higher grades. The abbreviated matrix shown in Figure 2.2, which was created through backloading, uses this approach. Another example is provided in Section III, Figure 3.15, with a more complete version of that same example on the CD.

    Regardless of the approach for selecting or writing objectives, tested objectives should be included in a district's scope and sequence well before those same objectives appear on state assessments so that students have adequate time for practice and mastery.

Figure 2.2

Abbreviated Sample of Backloaded Scope-and-Sequence Matrix (Tested objectives taken from an actual state curriculum document)

Concept	K	1	2	3
One-to-one	K.1.1A Use one-to-one corres-pondence and language such as more than, same number as, or two less than to describe relative sizes of sets of concrete objects.			
Concrete objects to represent numbers	K.1.1B Use sets of concrete objects to represent quantities given in verbal or written form (through 10).	1.1.1B Create sets of tens and ones using concrete objects to describe, compare, and order whole numbers.		
Compare and order place value *(Note multiple learning objectives within one objective at Grades 2 and 3. Discussion of this problem follows.)*		1.1.1A Compare and order whole numbers up to 99 (less than, greater than, or equal to) using sets of concrete objects and pictorial models.	2.1.1A Use concrete models to represent, compare, and order whole numbers (through 999), read the numbers, and record the comparisons using numbers and symbols (>, <, =).	3.1.1A Use place value to read, write (in numbers, expanded notation, symbols, and words), and describe the value of whole numbers through 999,999.
Compare and order place value *(Note multiple learning objectives within one objective. Discussion of this problem follows.)*				3.1.1B Use place value to compare and order whole numbers through 9,999, and read and write decimals up to tenths and hundredths, including money, using concrete models.

This format is crucial in identifying how objectives flow across grade levels. Frequently (but not always) state documents are created without writers from different grade levels talking to one another. As a result, there may be redundancy or gaps in the development of key concepts. The far left column (labeled Concepts, with names of concepts or skills chosen by the matrix creators) facilitates developing a flow in the matrix. You cannot depend upon state numbering systems to indicate spiraling development of the same concept. (E.g., Notice how 1.1.A and 1.1.B address different concepts from kindergarten to grade 3 in Figure 2.2.)

5. Add to the matrix any objectives determined by local needs, including any graduate profiles or expectations that may have been previously established. This is called frontloading.

6. Write precise, measurable objectives. Precision in writing depends upon the verb in use. Words such as "understand," "recognize," or "appreciate" do not describe what students should know or be able to do. Terms like "introduce" or "reinforce" speak to what the teacher will do. "Investigate" or "explore" can be student-learning activities, but those words fail to describe measurable student learning. Verbs and their contexts that communicate what the student learns and does might be: "define and give examples of," "identify," "explain in a three-paragraph response," "compare and contrast features of . . . in an oral presentation," "identify the . . . and evaluate the merits of each in consideration of . . .," or "construct a . . . using the principles of . . . ".

   Curriculum writers can use the following questions to measure quality of objectives.

   - Does the objective/indicator clearly state what the student will know or be able to do?
   - Does the objective focus on what students are to learn rather than on what the teacher will do?
   - Are objectives concise and easy to read?
   - Do I, as a classroom teacher, know what strategies I could use to teach this objective?
   - Do I know how I can assess student mastery of this objective?
   - Is the objective sufficiently clear that the teacher in the next room, looking at the same objective, will interpret its meaning in the same way that I do?

Some examples of objectives that match these criteria are given below.

- Generate a word problem from a given subtraction or addition sentence.
- Sort a collection of objects (such as attribute blocks) using a two-circle Venn diagram.
- Differentiate between renewable and nonrenewable energy sources in a brief single paragraph.

Poorly written objectives may include more than one instructional objective (as noted in the matrix), may include nonmeasurable terms (such as "understand"), and are often broad or lengthy. Examples of these include the following:

- Demonstrate knowledge of addition, subtraction, multiplication, and division; other number sense, including numeration and estimation; and the application of those operations.
- Demonstrate knowledge of mathematical systems (including real numbers, whole numbers, integers, fractions), geometry, and number theory.
- Understand natural selection, adaptation, and diversity.

7. Limit the number of objectives. Robert Marzano's research, as reported in *What Works in Schools*, has identified "a guaranteed and viable curriculum" as the most important factor in student learning (15, 22-34). "Guaranteed" means that all students have the opportunity to learn the same content—the written curriculum that all teachers are expected to deliver; "viable" means that the written curriculum is limited in scope to a number of objectives that teachers can expect students to master in the time available. A good rule of thumb for curriculum teams is the "100-80" rule: Plan a reasonable scope of content that will allow teachers to teach 100 percent of the content in 80 percent of the time available in the school year. Teaching 100 percent of the curriculum is not negotiable; if teachers do not teach 100 percent of the curriculum for any grade level or course, students enter the next grade with gaps in the knowledge that the receiving teacher expects them to have. The 80 percent time allocation, however, may vary from district to district; district personnel should agree on the time allocation that seems most reasonable to them. The "100-80" rule, or a district's modification of that rule, should allow for both re-teaching and enrichment, as well as taking into account those

instances when fire drills, pep assemblies, weather-related school cancellations, and other events eat into the teaching time.

The first draft will almost surely contain far more objectives than teachers can reasonably teach to mastery in a school year. Some specific steps and considerations can help the members of a curriculum development team reduce the number of objectives.

- Estimate the amount of time needed for students to master each objective, including time needed for distributed practice throughout the year. This should be a range (such as four to six hours), knowing that all students do not learn at the same rate. Estimates should be in hours rather than periods, as time allocations may vary from building to building. (Training activities for estimating time can be found in Section III, Figure 3.17.)
- Add the estimated time needed for mastery of all objectives (using the top end of the range) and compare that with the time available. Remember to use 80 percent of class time as the available teaching time; for example, if there are 180 class hours available, figure approximately 144 hours for actual teaching/learning time. (Your district may choose a percent other than 80 percent; if so, calculate from that percent.)
- When the estimated time exceeds the available time, cuts need to be made. If there are objectives in the matrix that do not appear on any external assessment, consider those for deletion. If all objectives are tested, then use information from item analysis of the state assessment to determine which objectives are tested more frequently (thus considered more important), and consider deleting less frequently tested ones. It is important to remember, however, that an objective not tested at one grade level may be prerequisite knowledge for an objective tested at a higher level.

Technology Tip

Work with the informational technology liaison to implement a relational database system that will establish connectivity across all phases of the work—scope-and-sequence development of, creation of curriculum guides, and writing and administration of assessments linked to specific assessments.

8. Classify the cognitive type of each objective. An example of classifying by cognitive type is provided in Section III, Figure 3.16. A rigorous set of objectives includes expectations across all cognitive

levels. A large percentage of objectives should be at the application level or more complex. Rewrite, as appropriate, those objectives for which expectations can be raised to higher levels, keeping in mind the assessment demands and instructional approaches intended.

9. Review and edit the draft document before sharing it with administrators, teachers, and other stakeholders across the district. Rewrite objectives for clarity if needed. If a verb says "understand," decide what you really want students to be able to do. Looking at a released test item related to the objective may provide insight. If an objective repeats across grade levels, decide how to spiral that objective so that the expectations for students increase across grade levels.

10. Disseminate the draft scope-and-sequence document to appropriate stakeholders, ensuring that you include in the review those teachers who will deliver the finalized curriculum. Make sure to clearly label the document DRAFT at this point. In soliciting feedback, you may want to include a brief questionnaire with the draft to guide individual or group reviews. Let teachers and others responding to the draft know that the team will consider all feedback, but that the final version may not reflect every suggestion. Establish a deadline for receiving and considering feedback. A sample questionnaire is included in Section III, Figure 3.18.

11. Consider all suggestions made and questions asked by reviewers when making final revisions to the scope-and-sequence document. Once finalized, the scope-and-sequence document now becomes the foundation for development of curriculum guides.

The scope-and-sequence document, as noted earlier, does not delineate when to address specific learning objectives within a given grade level or course. Once the scope-and-sequence document has been completed, district personnel may choose to create a pacing guide for each grade level or course that identifies the order in which objectives will be taught during the year. The time allocations determined in Step 7 on page 56 are helpful in this process. The pacing guide is not meant to prescribe day-by-day instruction; rather, it is meant to delineate content for larger chunks of time, such as months or grading periods. The synchronization provided by the process is especially helpful in districts with a mobile student population (students who move from one school to another within the district.) The caveat related to pacing guides is that they are just that—guides. Some students need more time than others to learn specific material. Teachers can address individual differences through differentiated instruction and extended learning time.

How To: Developing Curriculum Guides

Although there are some variations in procedural steps that might work well for teams charged with the responsibility for developing curriculum guides, the following approach has proven effective and practical in several districts. These steps elaborate upon the general steps contained in Section I, Curriculum Guides. The critical parameters to remember are that information contained in the guides should be clear and complete enough to support teachers in implementing the curriculum and using appropriate materials and instructional methods, but concise enough to avoid "overwhelming" the user. A good test is to ask a few questions: "Would this be meaningful and helpful to a new teacher who is learning the local curriculum and implementing it in the classroom?" "If I were given this guide, would I know enough to feel competent in planning my instruction for this subject area and grade level?" "Does this guide tell me enough about what students have been taught before they come to my classroom, if they have been in this school district?"

1. Prepare for guide development. Before work on specific curriculum guides begins, there are some broad, comprehensive steps to take that will apply to all curriculum review/development, documents, and processes. The district leadership should have put those into place with the comprehensive curriculum management policy referred to in the Overview and briefly outlined earlier: determining the format for guides and the content (see Section I, Curriculum Guides, Steps 5,); deciding whether the guides will be provided in hard copy or online; and clarifying the curriculum development process itself from the point of writing the scope-and-sequence documents through approval of the curriculum guides. If this foundation is not yet in place, consider the following parameters.

   A. Identify the desired components to be included in all curriculum guides, regardless of subject area. This should be done by the district leadership team. A typical example of components for curriculum guides follows but is not necessarily all-inclusive. The components agreed upon by the leadership team should be included on the guide pages for each curriculum objective. (See Section III, Figures 19-21 for tips on writing guides and for samples of curriculum guide pages.)

      • Learning goals and objectives obtained from the scope and sequence, clearly linked or keyed to state learning standards or frameworks, is the starting point for the written guides. These statements communicate what the students are expected to know and do.

- Information about *how* the students are expected to perform each objective is incorporated with each objective. E.g., "Given an unlabeled map of the Middle East, students will be able to identify the countries with 100 percent accuracy."

- Information estimating the typical timeframe for the learning should accompany each objective. This may also be included in a pacing chart for the subject area in the specific grade level.

- Clear statements of prerequisite skills/courses or expected prior mastery of skills need to be indicated for each objective. This information is found in the scope-and-sequence documents by reviewing objectives in the curriculum for grade levels or previous learning.

- Assessment information that keys each objective to the assessments (state or local) on which the students are held accountable for being able to demonstrate the knowledge or skills. Further, the guides should provide sample classroom assessment items. Ideally, the examples will represent different contextual approaches to the items—different cognitive levels, varying modes of questions. (See How To: Assessment Design and Development.)

- Identify the primary and supplemental instructional materials to use with each objective. Clear linkage between objectives and the content of instructional materials is a critical component to enhance use of the guides. Information from the instructional materials selection team is the critical informational resource for this information. (See How To: Instructional Materials Selection.)

- Provide specific examples of how to approach key concepts and skills relevant to each objective in the classroom. These examples make the guides especially helpful to teachers. There might be accompanying samples of activities, a list of activities, or suggested strategies for teachers to use.

B. Determine the appropriate format for presenting the agreed-upon guide contents. Consistency of format for the content among guides contributes to user-friendliness, so use of a predetermined, preferred format helps. A reasonable criterion for good guides is to make them useful for teachers and school administrators. This consideration is particularly important for elementary teachers who must use guides for several different curricular areas on a regular basis as they develop their lesson plans. Consistency of

guide formats also helps secondary teachers who teach more than one course or in more than one subject area. The scope-and-sequence documents developed by the curriculum teams are the foundation for developing the guides and should accompany each grade-level guide. Several issues need to be addressed in determining the format best for your district.

- Consider the adaptability of formats to all curricular areas.
- Collect some samples from other school districts or have a team member or two develop some examples of page layout options. (Guide format examples can be found in Figures 3.20 and 3.21 in Section III.)
- Determine whether the guides will be Web site-based curriculum documents or hard-copy versions. This decision is likely to influence the eventual choice of format.
- In general, avoid temptations to make the basic formats more than a maximum of two pages per objective. The guides do not need much narrative but do need clear topical information and clearly keyed cross-references.
- Come to consensus on the preferred format.
- Prepare a brief summary of the rationale for the selection and solicit feedback on the draft format from teachers not on the team.
- Make any modifications deemed appropriate based on that feedback.

2. Organize the team that will develop and write the guides.

- Confirm the timeline and calendar for the work in each curricular area being developed or reviewed and for which guides are being developed. Include review of resources, drafting of guide content, review of draft documents and feedback, required approvals by the board of education, production and distribution of guides, and training in use of guides as the critical actions in the process. Coordinate this scheduling with that of the instructional materials selection team. Include estimated times for ongoing follow-up training and annual training for teachers new to the district.

- Identify the team responsible for writing the guides (including at least some representation from the scope-and-sequence team, if not all members), and appoint a team leader to coordinate the work. This leader may be the same person who guided the scope-and-sequence document development, especially in smaller districts. Assign that role before the team convenes for the writing phase of work.

3. Provide staff development for the guide development/writing team.

- If team membership is expanded beyond those persons involved in developing the scope-and-sequence document, provide training or orientation to the tasks of writing guides as needed for the writing team based on their levels of expertise. The critical skills are outlined in How To: Scope and Sequence Development. (The need for training and skill development is one reason to try to retain the same team members from the scope-and-sequence work through the development of the guides.)
- If necessary, contract with a trainer for coaching in the skills of writing curriculum and designing guides. This effort will help to avoid confusion in the initial stages and enable the team members to move forward with confidence and complete the work efficiently.

4. Write the guides. Before beginning the work of writing the curriculum guides, it is preferred to have the scope-and-sequence team develop a preliminary pacing chart to identify estimated order and timing of instruction for the identified goals and objectives in the subject area(s) being addressed. (See How To: Scope and Sequence Development and Section III, Figure 3.22.) The chart development should consider when students are accountable for mastering the objectives included on state and local assessments, information that will be useful in later steps of curriculum guide writing. If this task has not been accomplished, it needs to be completed before moving further into this process.

- Using the chosen format, begin transferring the information available at this point into the designated component sections of the guides.
- Confirm that the content adequately matches state expectations for student learning content and curriculum document formats where that information is required and available.
- Be sure to identify instructional materials as "primary" and "supplemental," attending first to the primary materials adopted for the curricular area. The information contained in the forms for materials evaluation and selection may provide some of the important details regarding alignment with specific objectives. Assign one team member the specific duty of reviewing those evaluation forms for reference use.
- Invite teachers to contribute examples of effective classroom strategies or activities for the particular objectives where prior experience is identifiable. Add examples as needed, but continue to confirm their alignment with and appropriateness for the specific objectives.
- As the draft formats are completed for each subject area and grade level being addressed, review them for possible cross-references to such guide enclosures as a scope and sequence (K-12) and pacing charts for various grade levels and subject area objectives.

5. Obtain feedback and modify the draft.

- When a preliminary draft of a guide is available, assign team members to invite review and solicit feedback from teachers at school sites. Clarify that the writing team will consider, but might not include, all suggestions, based on the combined responses across schools.
- Document the feedback either with notes from team discussions or written feedback on the drafts returned by teachers after review.
- In addition to revisions indicated by feedback from teachers, revisions need to be made based on an in depth analysis of guide quality. Critical components to be considered for analysis include congruence of activities and assessments with objectives, distribution of objectives across cognitive types, and alignment of resources with objectives (including context and assessment formats). Additional components that might be considered are included in the Sample Curriculum Guide Analysis form, Section III, Figure 3.23. District personnel may choose to include other components that reflect local needs or priorities.
- Revise guide drafts as considered appropriate by the writing team.

6. Submit the guides for approval or adoption as required by district policy. Local policies and state requirements regarding board adoption of curriculum vary. Your requirements might dictate that the school board adopt/approve the scope-and-sequence documents for all curriculum, or that it adopt scope-and-sequence documents for elementary curriculum and course descriptions for secondary offerings. A few require board adoption of the actual curriculum guides for teachers. Your decisions on what documents will be taken to the local board for approval or adoption should conform to your own state law and local policy requirements.

- If policy requires that the school board approve only the scope-and-sequence documents laying out goals and objectives, the work moves to the implementation stage after this approval.
- If the policy requires that the school board approve both scope and sequence of goals/objectives and curriculum guides, prepare the guides for school board review and approval.
- If law or policy requires your board to approve course descriptions, those can be written simultaneously with completion of the scope-and-sequence documents or in conjunction with the writing of guides.

Should revisions be necessary after board review and before approval, amend as needed.

7. Disseminate the approved curriculum guides. After board approval, as dictated by law or policy, prepare guides for dissemination to all teachers, including scope-and-sequence information to support articulation needs. Begin the implementation of curricular changes and use of new instructional materials with staff development, and communicate curriculum information to parents in brief, user-friendly brochures, both in hard copy and on school and district Web sites. Retrieve all previous guides and communicate instructions to avoid their further use.

How To: Instructional Materials Selection

A school district should have a clearly outlined process for the selection of instructional materials to support delivery of the curriculum. Such a process includes not only steps for interacting with vendors of materials, but also clear steps and rubrics for evaluating the materials to ensure optimum alignment with the curriculum. Because the curriculum will have been aligned with state expectations, the result should be the availability of textbooks, supplemental books, software, and other resources that contribute directly to student mastery of the intended learning. With alignment as the driving force behind both curriculum design and materials selection, teachers will be better able to teach the adopted curriculum and to provide classroom instruction that lead students toward improved achievement.

Once the goals and objectives are prepared in a scope-and-sequence document, the materials selection can begin. Typically school board policy outlines the working relationship between the district and vendors/publishers of instructional materials; therefore, this guide will emphasize the process of evaluating and selecting the instructional materials.

If the school district is small and not likely to generate advantages by large-quantity purchasing, collaborating with nearby districts of similar size or through a service center/intermediate unit might be desirable to identify other potential purchasers who might benefit from meeting together with vendors and becoming part of a joint purchasing effort with your district. Regardless of that option, the following actions need to be undertaken.

1. Prepare for the work by determining logistics and organization of the process.

   • Choose a materials selection team. A district curriculum staff member, or in the absence of that option, a superintendent-appointed staff member with experience in curriculum materials review and analysis should lead the selection process. Principal recommendations and teacher applications can provide a pool of potential members for the team. (See sample forms in Section III, Figure 3.24.) The selection team should include representation from the group that developed the guides and representative teachers from all grade levels where the materials under review will be used. If the district is small enough to have each school represented without creating a cumbersome size for the team, that representation is a desirable end. In larger districts, designated team members might "represent" two or more schools during the process. Inclusion of a library media specialist on the team will provide expertise in locating resources for basic adoptions as well as supplemental resources.

- Establish and communicate the schedule for the team's work. Clearly designate periods of time for review and location of materials to be reviewed by interested staff members before the final selection is recommended to the school board. (Sample timelines are found in Section III, Figure 3.25.) Be sure to coordinate this schedule with the curriculum review cycle and the related curriculum review team's schedule.

- Identify the available instructional materials/textbooks suitable for consideration as the main support for delivery of the curriculum. Contact publishers and request samples of all related materials for review. Samples of correspondence are found in Section III, Figure 3.26.

- Establish a set of materials-review criteria and scoring forms as the expected guidelines for all materials-selection teams to use. (See example in Section III, Figure 3.27.) Include the curriculum goals, objectives, and any other information that communicates what students are expected to know or be able to do, as indicated in the scope-and-sequence document that has been aligned with assessments. The emphasis will be on evaluating the match/alignment of the materials' content with the topic of the learning (objective), the way in which the objective is to be learned and assessed, and the grade level in which the curriculum places the learning. The rubrics should also include factors such as readability and absence of culture, race, and gender biases.

- Conduct a review of the rubrics and put them into a form for practicing their use with sample materials.

- Undertake a team-wide inter-rater reliability check using the rubrics and form with at least two sample materials. Discuss results and identify problems that surfaced in variations of ratings by more than one point among team members. Determine whether the differences occurred from true differences of evaluation or from misunderstandings or inconsistent interpretations of the rubrics.

- Clarify or modify rubrics and further develop team consistency as needed in response to the reliability, and complete final draft of the rubrics and evaluation forms.

2. Conduct the preliminary materials evaluation. These steps will narrow the field of publishers and products for final review.

- Have team members work individually, each studying the materials and completing independent rating sheets.
- When the initial rating sheets have been completed, the team leader should review the ratings and identify any materials and elements of curriculum in which there were variances of more than one point among the raters on the criteria. These will be the topics of the first post-rating group discussion.
- Discuss the variances among team members to determine the rationale underlying individuals' ratings and reach consensus ratings of no more than one point variation on total ratings if possible.
- Tabulate the results into a summary form to provide a composite of all ratings. (See sample in Section III, Figure 3.27.) It is recommended that you not average these ratings, but rather that you record the numbers of each rating and the total points (e.g., 7 - 3s, 5 - 2s [31]). Keeping track of the numbers of each rating can preclude recalculation work if questions or disagreements arise later.
- Review the team members' composite results and discuss the materials, one publisher/vendor at a time, to ensure that team members note and understand any questions related to areas of alignment and gaps in alignment.
- Develop a final tabulation of ratings from the earlier forms with modifications that individuals wish to submit based on the team discussion. Retain these forms for use in developing curriculum guides so that references to instructional resources can include specific information regarding location of alignment with objectives or the absence of linkage. If no linkage is present, supplemental resources will need to be identified in the guide.
- The team leader identifies the ranking of vendors/materials according to the rating results and presents the results for full team approval.
- The team determines how many vendors to move forward in consideration for adoption and then, according to the district procedures, solicits multiple copies of materials for further review or piloting.

3. Pilot the materials if piloting has been predetermined as a step in the process. Some school districts choose to ask a team of teachers to pilot use of the tentative selections based on ratings before they proceed with publisher interviews and development of a single recommendation for further consideration. Others proceed with the next steps and then pilot the tentative first-choice selection. Still others complete the evaluation process and do not include a piloting stage.

For those who choose to include a piloting stage, sample letters and information are included in Section III, Figure 3.28.

4. Select publishers to interview, conduct the interviews, and review results with staff.

A. With team approval of the rankings as summarized, the team selects the tentatively favored materials, typically the highest rated materials and the next one or two. However, do not include those with ratings substantially lower than the most highly rated materials unless district policy or procedures require a set number of vendors to be interviewed. Sample forms for summarizing review ratings are in Section III, Figure 3.29.

B. Schedule individual times for interviews with the vendor/publisher representatives for the one to three "favored materials." Invite them for the interview meetings with the team for the clear purpose of establishing several additional pieces of information and options for consideration as the final decision is made. Sample interview questions are found in Section III, Figure 3.26. Conduct the interview sessions. While this process must be guided by any prescribed procedures in local board policy related to district/vendor relations, the following are typical actions.

• Hold separate sessions with representatives from the publishers in the "final" top rankings.
• Focus on such factors as price breaks, initial and follow-through training and support service available to new users of the materials, supplemental materials available with the primary materials (e.g., CDs, videos), and delivery schedules.
• Obtain written information to confirm details or "agreements" made in the oral interviews prior to your decision on materials to be recommended.

C. After interview meetings are concluded, reconvene the team to determine the recommended materials to propose for staff review and potential board approval. The team may wish to select a primary recommendation at this point if there is a clear delineation of preference by scoring and by staff comments. Then invite that publisher to do a formal presentation and answer questions at an open meeting. Otherwise, you may wish to simply continue consideration of the favored two or three and invite those publishers to make presentations at separate meetings. A sample letter to publisher representatives to follow interviews appears in Figure 3.26 on the CD. Provide time for staff review of the materials and a summary of the team's evaluation work. You may accomplish this through either site-based reviews or an invitational review and discussion time period for any administrators and teachers interested in reviewing the recommended materials, seeing the evaluation results, and discussing the recommendation with team members before preparing a recommendation for the superintendent and school board. Ensure the availability of sufficient copies of the materials under consideration so that they can be made available at the school sites for staff discussions during this period. In accordance with your district policy regarding review of instructional materials before adoption, also advertise a schedule of times for parents or other interested community members to review and comment on the documents. Include team members during those periods as much as possible so that questions might be answered. Teachers who review the materials should be asked to complete a rating sheet using the established rubrics used by the original raters.

D. Invite the finalist publisher(s) to make presentations in the district and to answer questions as part of the next level of review. Include teacher response forms as a follow-up to these presentations. (See Section III, Figure 3.27, or use rubric evaluation sheets from earlier steps.)

5. Make the recommendation for adoption.

• Make a team decision on the materials to be recommended to the superintendent and board. The decision-making process should take into consideration the staff response forms, the team's evaluation data, the information gleaned from the publishers' interviews and presentations, and any additional information developed to this stage. A form for summarizing the cost analysis information for this step is included in Figure 3.29 on the CD. Earlier rating summary sheets are appropriate for use at this stage as well.

- Prepare a formal report for the superintendent and board recommending the materials to be adopted and subsequently purchased. Include the key points of evaluation and the rationale for the selection.
- Finalize school board approval for adoption of the materials to be used in implementing the curriculum.

6. Move from adoption to use of materials.

   A. Assign to a small follow-up team the responsibility of supporting the search for supplemental materials where such needs have been designated for specific learning objectives during the materials rating process. This team should:

   - Solicit all teachers' suggestions for the specific supplemental needs so that teachers are aware of the needs and can become part of the effort to meet those needs.
   - Conduct some alignment checks with the supplemental materials consistent with the approach used in choosing primary materials.
   - Provide a list and briefing to the materials selection team and seek their approval of the optional, supplementary materials list for use by schools as desired.
   - Disseminate the list to all principals and teachers in the curriculum areas involved.

   B. Provide staff development in implementation of the curriculum (as included in the scope and sequence and eventually in the written guides) and in use of the adopted materials over several weeks or months. (See Sample Staff Development Calendar in Section III, Figure 3.33.) Offer follow-up assistance from either school district personnel or a team of school-based staff who have been intensely trained in use of the materials and can become the "in-house" experts to support teachers as needed. To ensure common understanding of the curriculum and materials, it is recommended that all teachers and librarians be required to attend "preparation" training sessions; supportive follow-up sessions can be voluntary. The initial "preparation" sessions are best held in grade level teams, or in subject/course teams at the secondary level. The voluntary training sessions can be held by grade level or in articulation teams of teachers and librarians within a school or across schools.

C. Establish periodic "debriefing" sessions in which teachers can discuss any problems that arise in implementation of the curriculum using the adopted and supplemental materials. (See How To: Curriculum Monitoring.) Use the information from these discussions to inform decisions about further staff development, assistance to teachers, or curriculum modification needs. Retain the process and use of the adopted materials through the time period consistent with the curriculum review cycle.

How To: Assessment Design and Development

The creation and use of high quality assessments—at both the district and classroom levels—is crucial to the promotion of student learning, to the identification of what students have and have not learned, to the reporting of the status of student learning, and to the selection of interventions to remediate learning deficiencies. Staff development should be provided for all personnel with assessment responsibilities. Beyond staff development, there are specific steps to follow or considerations to address in order to offer quality assessment opportunities for students. A timeline sample to address this work is found in Section III, Figure 3.30, as is a planning guide in Figure 3.31.

1. Provide staff development for all personnel with assessment responsibilities (including classroom teachers) that includes the following components:

   • a variety of methods for assessment—such as observation, check lists, constructed response, multiple choice, and performance tasks—and when each method is most appropriate;
   • specific examples of ways to use observations and checklists;
   • writing questions that match identified learning objectives;
   • writing good multiple choice questions, including effective stems, good distracters, and parallel format for distracters;
   • writing performance tasks with scoring guidelines;
   • writing questions that require different levels of cognitive skills (knowledge, application, analysis); and
   • user-friendly format for tests, with all the same types of questions

together and appropriate use of white space and page arrangement to reduce chances for distraction or confusion.

If expertise in assessment methodology does not exist within the district, district personnel might want to take advantage of external workshops that are available in this area. Some workshops provide trainer-of-trainer materials that can be used in participants' home districts to build capacity of staff members across the district.

Technology Tip

Link work in assessment development with a relational database system that connects all assessment items with specific objectives.

Timing for staff development related to using appropriate assessment methods and creating high-quality written assessments is important. Knowledge from staff development that takes place too far in advance of actual writing tends to grow stale so that time to reactivate that knowledge is required.

2. Create district- and building-level assessments using the following steps:

- Select the specific learning objectives from the district's written curriculum that will be included on a given assessment. (See sample text specifications for a quarterly test in Section III, Figure 3.32.) Objectives selected should reflect the emphasis of the state assessment, but not be restricted to objectives included on that test. Results from state assessments should also be considered when selecting objectives to be included on local assessments; areas in which district students show particular weakness are ones that should be emphasized on any district tests.
- Identify the assessment method or methods that will be used, taking into consideration the way scoring will be done. Requiring students to respond in a variety of ways increases the likelihood those same students will be prepared for any type of external assessment; this is one important aspect of deep alignment.
- Determine the length of the assessment and the number of questions related to each learning objective.
- Write questions to meet established parameters of the assessment.
- Review questions, based on assessment results, to determine revisions or modifications that will make the test more valid and more reliable.

- If you plan to administer specific tests repeatedly over time, establish appropriate security measures. If you will add new items for subsequent assessments of the same learning objectives, determine how an item bank can be developed with parallel items at the same level of difficulty; this will allow for comparability of results over time.

How To: Staff Development and Implementation of a New or Revised Curriculum

With a scope-and-sequence document and curriculum guides in place and instructional materials selected, focus now turns to strategies for effective implementation. The importance of staff development was emphasized in the sections on needs assessment, scope and sequence, materials selection, curriculum development, and assessment design and development. Likewise, staff development is a critical component of the work involved in effective implementation of a new or revised curriculum.

Even in the event that the district administration has determined that development of guides will immediately follow design of the scope and sequence and selection of materials, implementation still proceeds at this juncture with staff development related to the scope and sequence and materials selected instead of waiting for the completion of guides. In that instance, the further development of guides is an evolving work, expanding the contents that support the curriculum implementation and refining information available to teachers to ensure alignment of a written, taught, and tested curriculum. Phasing in curriculum guide review and adoption, along with eventual full use of the guides, occurs as the documents are completed. Under either approach to the timing and ordering of steps, the following actions need to be included in implementation:

1. Identify a district curriculum leader (or in the absence of such a position, identify a superintendent-appointed staff member with curriculum leadership skills) to direct and coordinate the implementation work.

2. Establish a plan and schedule for principal and teacher staff development and follow-through support using the completed scope-and-sequence matrix, the curriculum guides (if prepared by this juncture), and the accompanying instructional materials selected for the new curriculum.

3. To ensure common understanding of the curriculum and materials, it is recommended that all teachers and principals be required to attend "preparation" training sessions in the curricular areas of their instruction or supervision; supportive follow-up sessions can be voluntary. The initial "preparation" sessions might be held in district-wide or school-based grade level teams, or in subject/course teams at the secondary level. The voluntary training sessions can be held by grade level or in vertical teams of teachers within a school or across schools. (See Sample Staff Development Calendar excerpts in Section III, Figure 3.33.)

4. Disseminate the new curriculum documents (scope-and-sequence matrix or curriculum guides, and new instructional materials). Distribution can be either in advance of the training sessions to allow for preview or during the sessions to provide contextual framework and common explanations to all staff in the same setting.

5. Plan for and communicate availability of follow-up assistance to teachers as they implement the curriculum and use the adopted materials. The resource persons for this assistance can be from either school district personnel or a team of school-based staff who have been intensely trained in use of the materials and are the "in-house" experts to support teachers. The assistance might be offered to groups of teachers at the school sites (e.g., grade level teams or subject area teams) or to individual teachers as determined by assessment of the varying staff needs after the preparation training sessions.

6. Include within the staff development training and follow-up assistance several development activities for principals and any other persons responsible for coaching and monitoring curriculum implementation. Including principals with their teacher teams in curriculum training (Step #3 above) is desirable both to foster the team approach to implementation and to communicate the message that principals will be an ongoing source of guidance, monitoring, support, and accountability for use of the new curriculum and instructional materials.

7. Either at this point or in conjunction with the finalization of curriculum guides, write brief brochures that explain the new curriculum to parents and communicate the student learning expectations within the curriculum. (See Sample Parent Brochure in Section III, Figure 3.34.)

8. Disseminate the curriculum brochures widely among parents to optimize their understanding and awareness of the curricular changes. Consider district- or school-based mini-sessions to further explain the curriculum, answer parent questions, and communicate the future actions related to assessment and evaluation as part of the curriculum management system.

Technology Tip

Let parents know what kind of information is available to them on school and district Web sites. Don't neglect to communicate the same information through newsletters and parent meetings.

9. Communicate the desired procedures for staff to offer ongoing feedback or questions related to curriculum implementation so that information is not lost during the interim between stages of implementation and review and revision. One common strategy for this step is to encourage teachers to retain implementation notes and to either schedule periodic "debriefing" sessions or invite periodic staff submission of suggestions for modification during the next review and revision activities.

10. When planning future staff development and support activities related to curriculum delivery, consider the questions and suggestions that surface during implementation in order to promote continuous improvement of both curriculum and instruction.

How To: Curriculum Monitoring

Curriculum monitoring assists in establishing an ethic of consistent improvement in the delivery of the curriculum. The primary responsibility for monitoring the delivery of the specified curriculum rests with the building principal. An effective principal provides leadership aimed at diagnosing instructional behaviors, improving teaching, and continuously reviewing expected teaching of the district-adopted curriculum and the accompanying instructional materials. Monitoring needs to be systematic and occur at all levels to ensure that the board-adopted curriculum is being implemented in a way the system has established. Written documents need to clarify district expectations for principals and other instructional supervisors to assist and support them in monitoring the curriculum.

Fundamental to sound curriculum monitoring is the presence of a clearly delineated process that includes teacher planning guides. (See sample in Section III, Figure 3.35 and Figure 3.36.) Developing an effective process for monitoring the curriculum involves the following steps:

1. Establish expectations for monitoring the delivery of the curriculum on a consistent basis. Some districts accomplish this through the principals' annual goal getting. Specific steps to consider include the following:

   • Establish goals for building administrators and central office administrators with responsibilities for curriculum and instruction relative to time spent on curriculum monitoring. If improvement is to occur, building administrators should work toward the ultimate goal of spending 35 to 50 percent of their time in classrooms.
   • Develop or revise building level and appropriate central office administrative job descriptions to include responsibility for monitoring the delivery of the board-adopted curriculum.
   • Establish criteria linking administrative evaluations to classroom monitoring practices.
   • Develop policies or written processes that include requirements for building-level administrators to monitor the implementation of the approved curriculum.

2. Plan and implement administrative training on an ongoing basis to meet the expectations established for the monitoring of the curriculum. The training should include any employee who has responsibilities for making sure that the curriculum is delivered so that all students have equal access to it. Identify and implement a consistent administrator training process in the area of classroom observations. Identify a specific observation and feedback process that will assist administrators in gathering data while observing in classrooms and delivering feedback to teachers.

The Downey walk-through model described in *The Three-Minute Classroom Walk-Through* provides a strong research-based collaborative system for curriculum monitoring that is not evaluative in nature. The observation structure focuses on the gathering of data in five designated areas (20-36) in a short two-to-four minute period of time in the classroom. The model also allows for attention to school or district expectations as well as implementation of specific programs.

Using the data collected in the classroom, the observer decides whether or not to provide feedback to the teacher. Because of the short duration of the observation, an observer may base feedback on several classroom observations rather than a single one. Feedback can be direct in nature, or it can encourage teachers to self-reflect on their curriculum implementation and teaching practices (Downey, 43-81).

Other specific strategies that might reinforce effective curriculum monitoring could include a review of lesson plans, samples of materials that teachers distribute to students as part of the instructional process, and formative assessments given to students. These reviews would focus on alignment with the district curriculum and district/state assessment objectives. Teachers' systematic feedback to principals and curriculum administrators can also be useful. (See Curriculum/Textbook Feedback Form in Section III, Figure 3.37.) Analysis of instructional materials and formal assessments provides information about the match between these materials and the learning objectives as well as the level of cognition required for students to complete the work, whether classroom instruction or formal assessment. (See sample teacher and principal forms for linkage of student work to standards and objectives in Section III, Figures 3.38 and 3.39.)

How To: Assessment Implementation and Data Use

A successful district-wide assessment program depends upon four key ingredients: an overall assessment plan that guides all assessment and evaluation within the district, well-designed assessments with items that specifically match student learning expectations, ethical and consistent test administration, and appropriate use of data derived from the assessments. The "How To" sections for the Comprehensive Assessment Plan and Assessment Design and Development have addressed the first two considerations. The steps that follow describe the considerations relevant to test administration and use of data. The steps apply specifically to district-wide administration, but many of them are applicable to teacher-made assessments as well.

1. Determine how to score assessments and make appropriate purchases of hardware or supplies needed for this purpose.

2. Once content-area assessments have been designed, arrange for duplication and dissemination of the assessments at the appropriate time. Duplication procedures may vary depending upon security requirements. If a test is to remain secure, print and distribute the test at a district site, with the requirement that tests be returned. If security is not an important issue, you might share master copies of tests electronically, with personnel at each building having the responsibility for duplicating the assessment. In the latter case, building personnel may need budgetary support for the duplication costs.

3. Develop clear and specific instructions for the administration that will accompany each test.

4. Provide staff development relative to purposes for assessment and assessment protocol for all teachers and building administrators, as well as any district administrators with curriculum and assessment responsibilities.

5. Once tests have been administered, score tests in the predetermined method.

6. If tests are scored at the district level, provide feedback in user-friendly format that includes information about the following:

   - performance of total groups by class, grade level, building, and district;
   - performance of individual students;
   - performance by objective, tied back to the learning objectives for the subject and grade level being tested; and
   - disaggregated performance of any subgroup of students of

Technology Tip

Work with informational technology personnel to develop a scoring and reporting system that will provide relevant data in a user-friendly format. The structure of such a system needs to be considered when the comprehensive assessment plan is developed.

significant size. The size of the group would be predetermined by district personnel.

It should be noted that a separate report might not be necessary for each of the categories above. Reports might be formatted in such a way that multiple results could be gleaned from the same report. (See sample Computer Report in Section III, Figure 3.40.)

7. If teachers are expected to score tests, provide appropriate forms for tallying and organizing data. Provide teachers with the time and training needed to do this. (See sample hand-analysis forms in Section III, Figures 3.42 and 3.43.)

8. Provide staff development in the appropriate interpretation of the data (regardless of how it was scored) and how to use the data to guide curricular and instructional decision-making. (See Ten Tips for Using Data Effectively in Section III, Figure 3.44.)

The ability to present data in a meaningful and usable form is not an innate skill. It requires an understanding of the foundations behind the data and the ways in which data will be used. At the user end, many professional educators have not received formal training in the use of data. If outside assistance is needed in planning for the presentation of data and initial staff development in the use of data, seek that outside help. Do so, however, with the intention of building internal capacity to sustain the processes of data presentation and analysis. (See a sample data mentors program outline in Section III, Figure 3.45.)

How To: Program Evaluation

Program evaluation, within a public school context, is the process of systematically determining the quality of a curriculum in a given content area or any other school program and how the quality of that program might be improved. Program evaluation has a variety of purposes: to identify needs to set priorities, to identify appropriate methods for designing and implementing a program, to monitor and adjust during implementation, to determine whether a program is meeting desired outcomes, and to modify or terminate existing programs.

The process of evaluation includes determining the criteria by which a process will be evaluated and the data needed for those criteria, actually gathering the data, and then applying the criteria to the data to determine the status of the program. There are specific steps that provide the framework for almost any evaluation that a district might undertake. District personnel should establish such a framework to guide action planning for any program evaluation. The following steps provide a prototype for such a framework.

1. Describe the purpose of the evaluation by answering critical questions.

   • Why do you want to evaluate this program?
   • What led to this decision?
   • What problem do you expect to solve or what questions do you expect to answer as a result of the evaluation?

2. Define the parameters of the program to be evaluated.

   • Determine the scope of the program evaluation. Is it district, building, or grade level?
   • Delineate components of the program that will be included in the evaluation.
   • Decide in advance if program personnel will be evaluated as part of the total program evaluation. If personnel are to be included, make sure the processes involved are consistent with any negotiated agreement with the teachers' association.

3. Outline a management plan. (See an evaluation plan template and a sample of a completed evaluation in Section III, Figures 3.46 and 3.47.)

   • Identify a team leader, as well as additional personnel who will be involved in the evaluation process. Delineate any requirements for these personnel as well as ways of selecting them (voluntary, nomination).
   • Determine data to be used and methods for collection and analysis.
   • Identify appropriate criteria for evaluating the collected data.
   • Develop a timeline that is realistic in terms of time constraints of personnel involved and the data that are to be gathered. Include periodic team meetings in that timeline.
   • Identify resources that will be needed and allocate funds to support those needs.

- Assign responsibilities.

4. Plan how the results will be used.

- Develop an appropriate reporting format for the results.
- Determine who will see these results and how the results will be shared.
- Decide in advance the range of follow-up actions that might be taken as a result of the evaluation. Actions could range from termination to maintaining the status quo with no action to be taken. A more likely action in most cases would be development of a specific action plan to modify the program to improve its effectiveness in meeting stated goals.

With a district-established program evaluation format in place, a specific program evaluation can be initiated in any area. The designated team leader for the evaluation will oversee the following steps, which reflect the process described above.

- Write a formal program evaluation action plan, describing the process from beginning to end as it applies to the program under consideration.
- Conduct the evaluation, including compilation and analysis of data.
- Formulate recommendations.
- Communicate results and recommendations to the predetermined audience and decision makers. (See sample executive summary in Section III, Figure 3.48.)

Technology Tip

The template for program evaluation should be online and easily accessible for anyone who will have responsibility for program evaluation. Final evaluation reports should also be stored online and be available to appropriate district personnel.

Designation of responsibility for recommendations that flow from the program evaluation will be determined by the nature of the recommendations. Establish a follow-up plan for dealing with recommendations, including periodic updates from designated personnel as part of the plan.

Figure 2.3
Task-Tracking Matrix for Basic Steps in the "Nuts and Bolts" Section II

Step and Task	Leader	Completion Date Target	Actual Completion Date
Needs Assessment			
Select team			
Confirm timeline for development of plan			
Write the plan			
Provide preview and comment time for appropriate staff			
Submit to Superintendent and Board for approval			
Curriculum Development Cycle Planning			
Establish a curriculum development/review cycle coordinated with necessary state cycles			
Assessment Plan Development			
Select team for assessment planning and writing			
Confirm timeline for plan development			
Scope and Sequence Development			
Designate a leader and select the team			
Provide needs assessment and data reports to team			
Train team members			
Design matrix for entering standards and broad goals/outcomes			
Write objectives aligned with standards and place into a matrix			
Classify cognition domains for prioritized objectives and modify as needed			
Review objectives for allocation of estimated time requirements			
Provide review and comment time for feedback from staff			
Consider comments and finalize document for appropriate approvals/adoption			
Curriculum Guide Development			
Adopt a common guide format and contents/components, determination of publication method (online or hard copy or both)			
Clarify the intended process for writing and completing the guides			
Organize the guide development/team(s) ✓ Confirm timeline and calendar for the work of each area under review ✓ Coordinate timeline with materials selection team ✓ Identify the leader and team members for this next stage of work			

Step and Task	Leader	Completion Date Target	Actual Completion Date
Provide additional staff development for the team members if necessary			
Gather necessary documents: scope-and-sequence document, assessment information (state and district)			
Distribute scope-and-sequence document			
Invite teachers to submit model lessons or suggested strategies and classroom activities for any objectives they are interested in supporting			
Complete curriculum guide drafts			
Seek required approvals of guide drafts			
Disseminate approved guides to teachers			
Prepare for staff development and implementation			
Instructional Materials Selection			
Choose the materials selection team			
Identify and collect the available materials/textbooks for consideration			
Establish an agreed upon set of criteria for evaluation of materials (if not already established in your district) and put rubrics into forms for use in evaluation			
Conduct inter-rater reliability checks before proceeding with evaluations			
Conduct the evaluations, individually first and then by group discussion of rating results from individual work after tabulation of scores			
Resolve differences as needed and identify the preferential ranking of materials			
Determine how many publishers should be considered			
Select the publishers for interviews based on the ratings, and schedule interviews			
Conduct interviews of publishers			
Determine the team's tentative recommendations and provide time for staff to review the materials and provide feedback to the team			
Invite finalist publisher(s) to make presentations and answer questions			
Prepare report and recommendation to superintendent and board for adoption of materials per board policy and administrative regulations of your district			
Prepare staff development on use of the adopted materials with the local curriculum			

Step and Task	Leader	Completion Date Target	Actual Completion Date
Assessment Design and Development			
Plan and provide staff development needed for personnel with assessment responsibilities			
Select the learning objectives from the scope and sequence that will be assessed and when the assessments will occur			
Identify the appropriate assessment methods/items for each objective			
Confirm parallelism or similarities to types of assessments that will be required of students on high-stakes assessments			
Write the assessment questions/items			
Review drafts and revise as needed			
Establish appropriate security if tests are to be used repeatedly over time			
Determine how an item bank will be established and secured if new items will be included over time			
Staff Development and Curriculum Implementation			
Designate the implementation coordinator			
Disseminate guides, including scope and sequence, and materials to teachers			
Plan staff development for teachers, principals, assistant principals, and district staff as needed in using the new curriculum and materials			
Plan periodic follow-through sessions and support activities			
Write brochures to explain new or revised curriculum to parents and plan communication methods			
Develop and implement a mechanism for teachers to provide continuing feedback on curriculum and materials implementation			
Curriculum Monitoring			
Establish clear expectations regarding curriculum monitoring			
Plan staff development for principals, assistant principals, and any district staff to be involved in monitoring curriculum implementation and supporting teachers' use of new curriculum and materials			
Develop forms for monitoring activities			
Establish ongoing follow-up support			
Identify key points in the year for feedback on monitoring observations from administrators and teachers			

Step and Task	Leader	Completion Date Target	Actual Completion Date
Assessment Implementation and Data Use			
Determine how assessments will be scored			
Develop clear instructions for administration of each assessment			
Provide staff development for building principals, teachers, and relevant district staff regarding appropriate and ethical use of the assessments			
Score tests			
Design feedback for post-scoring dissemination			
Analyze performance of total groups (district, school, grade level, class)			
Analyze performance of individual students			
Analyze performance by questions (tied back to objectives)			
Disaggregate performance data of any subgroup of students of significant size			
Provide staff development in appropriate interpretation of data and application to decision-making for curricular and for classroom instructional purposes			
Program Evaluation			
Identify the purpose of the evaluation			
Define the parameters of the program to be evaluated			
Outline a plan for the evaluation			
Plan how results will be used and by whom			
Conduct the evaluation			
Communicate results and recommendations to the pre-determined decision-makers			
Act on recommendations			

Section III • Sample Forms and Letters

All of the material included in this section is also contained on the CD that accompanies this book. Files on the CD are frequently more extensive than the examples found in this section. Figure numbers for files on the CD match the figure numbers that are referenced in Section II.

Index of Figures and Accompanying CD Files

Needs Assessment

Figure 3.1 is a sample needs assessment survey that can be sent out at an appropriate time so that data will be available for the needs assessment team to consider.

Figure 3.2 is an actual summary of responses from a needs assessment conducted by one district.

Figure 3.3 is a sample of a prioritized list of data and materials that a needs assessment team might assemble to guide its work.

Figure 3.1

XYZ SCHOOL DISTRICT
MEMORANDUM
(Sample needs assessment memo to teachers in content area being addressed.)

To: K-12 Social Studies Teachers
From: Dr. Beverly Greene, Curriculum Director
Re: Social Studies Curriculum Revision
Date: April XX, XXXX

To prepare for the social studies revision process next year, we invite all social studies instructors to complete the following needs assessment. The answers to the following questions will guide the development of program goals. Please return to Dr. Greene at the administration building by May 15.

Grade Level or Course _____

1. What are the main themes of social studies in your grade/course in the present curriculum?

2. Do objectives appear to match your students' needs?

3. From your perspective, do district objectives align with state expectations?

4. What should be added to the current curriculum?

5. What should be removed from the current curriculum?

6. Other comments.

Figure 3.2

XYZ SCHOOL DISTRICT
MEMORANDUM
(Sample social studies needs assessment survey data memo to teachers)

To: K-6 Social Studies Teachers
From: Dr. Beverly Greene, Curriculum Director
Re: Social Studies Needs Assessment Data
Date:

Included is a summary of K-6 results from the needs assessment surveys that were sent out in May. We received responses from 61 percent of the 348 elementary K-6 classroom teachers.

Grade	# Responding	Responses
K	31	36% - more focus on family
1	26	34% - add family, neighborhood focus 56% - eliminate focus on Native Americans
2	33	42% - reduce number of countries/continents studied 30% - want a textbook
3	34	38% - increase map and geography activities 70% - want a textbook
4	25	33% - eliminate focus on Native South Americans 56% - want a textbook
5	24	24% - increase map skills 40% - satisfied with current curriculum
6	37	24% - increase map skills 41% - reduce number of cultures studied

Figure 3.3

Sample Prioritized List of Data Sources for Needs Assessment
(determined by team after identifying information sources)

1. Mission statements of district, schools, and units within the district operations

2. Student assessment data:

   ✓ State testing – disaggregated by school, grade level, special program enrollment (special education, English as a Second Language, Gifted/Talented), socio-economic status, ethnicity, and gender
   ✓ Statewide assessment results comparing our district with similar districts
   ✓ District tests—all grades tested—disaggregated by school, grade level, special program enrollment (special education, English as a Second Language, Gifted/Talented), socio-economic status, ethnicity, and gender
   ✓ Disaggregated assessment information (item analysis) that identifies types of questions or specific questions and student performance on those items

3. Current district strategic or long-range plan and school/district improvement plans

4. School/District Report Cards (most recent three years)

5. *No Child Left Behind* information regarding status and required improvements

6. State standards and information regarding anticipated changes

7. State assessment information (current and planned assessment calendars and related requirements, statewide assessment data)

8. State requirements regarding instructional materials/textbooks adoption

9. Board policies related to curriculum development, assessment, materials selection, and staff development

10. Attendance data—disaggregated by school, grade level, socio-economic status, ethnicity, and gender

11. Community demographics by socio-economic and ethnicity—past three years and projected five to 10 years

Curriculum Development/Review Cycle

File Name   **Content**
Figure 3.4   Curriculum Revision and Materials Adoption Cycle
Figure 3.5   Curriculum Revision Process (by year)
Figure 3.6   K-12 Curriculum Revision Cycle
Figure 3.7   K-12 Curriculum Revision Cycle and Textbook Adoption Plan
Figure 3.8   Curriculum Revision Timeline

Figure 3.4 and **Figure 3.5** provide two different overviews of a six-year revision cycle, without any reference to specific curriculum areas.

Figure 3.6 and **Figure 3.7** are examples of six-year cycles in which specific content areas are identified.

Figure 3.8 provides a schedule for the first year of curriculum revision in a specific content area.

Figure 3.4

XYZ School District
Sample Curriculum Revision and Materials Adoption Cycle

Six-Year Revision Cycle

Year 1	Year 2	Year 3	Year 4	Year 5	Year 6
Develop	Adopt & Implement	Monitor	Monitor	Monitor & Evaluate	Monitor/ Plan

Revision Cycle Procedures

	Procedure	Suggested Timeline
1.	Identify Curriculum Area for Revision	Fall (year 1)
2.	Evaluate Existing Curriculum (Needs Assessment) • Identify national and state outcomes • Identify local concerns (Community, Schools)	Spring (year 1)
3.	Establish Curriculum Revision Committee	Spring (year 1)
4.	Develop Program Mission and Goals • Create Scope and Sequence • Create Curriculum Guides	Summer (year 1)
5.	Review/Correlate Instructional Materials	Summer (year 1)
6.	Preview Instructional Materials Review/evaluation Curriculum Guide Drafts	Fall (year 2)
7.	Validate/revise Curriculum Guides	Fall (year 2)
8.	Select Instruction Materials	Winter (year 2)
9.	Begin Staff Inservice	Winter (year 2)
10.	Develop Content Assessments	Spring (year 2)
11.	Implement Districtwide	Fall (year 3)
12.	Review of Program (Program Evaluation)	Spring (years 3-6)

Figure 3.5

XYZ School District

Curriculum Revision Process
Six-year Cycle

Year 1 **Needs Assessment**

- Identify Curriculum Area
- Evaluate Student Results
- Consider State and National Standards
- Consider Local Indicators

Year 2 **Curriculum Revision**

- Organize Revision Writing Team
- Develop Curriculum Mission, Goals, and Strands
- Write Learner Objectives
- Create Written Scope and Sequence
- Validate Curriculum Internally: Committee
- Validate Curriculum Externally: Teaching Staff
- Write Curriculum Guides

Year 3 **Instructional Materials - Staff Development**

- Correlate Instructional Materials Selections: Long List
- Preview Instructional Materials: Short List
- Select Instructional Materials
- Order Materials
- Begin Staff Development

Year 4 **Implementation of Curriculum**

- Implement Revised Curriculum
- Continue Staff Development
- Monitor Program
- Solicit Feedback

Years 5-6 **Continue Implementation of Curriculum**

Figure 3.6

XYZ School District
Sample K - 12 Curriculum Revision Cycle

Year of Implementation	Content Areas	
Year 1	• Reading/Language Arts: K-12 • Family and Consumer Science	• Spanish 1 • Latin 1 • French 1 • German 1
Year 2	• Mathematics: K-12	• Spanish 2 • French 2 • Latin 2 • German 2
Year 3	• Science: K-12 • Health • Physical Education • Driver's Education	• Spanish 3 • French 3 • Latin 3 • German 3
Year 4	• Social Studies: K-12	• French 4 • German 4 • Spanish 4 • Latin 4
Year 5	• Business • Music	• Spanish 5 • French 5
Year 6	• Art • Industrial Technology	• Spanish 6 • French 6

Note: International Language revisions are phased in concurrently across languages because of the principles and strategies of language development. A consistent, systematic approach to building vocabulary and teaching/learning of syntax is essential and will be highly correlated with the textbook that is adopted. As a result, one textbook series may need to be identified in Year 1 that best meets the needs of the entire sequence of courses, with subsequent curriculum phase-ins and textbook purchases in years that follow.

Figure 3.7

XYZ School District
Sample K-12 Curriculum Revision Cycle and Textbook Adoption Plan
(Draft Proposal)

Revision Cycle

Year 1	Year 2	Year 3	Year 4	Year 5	Year 6
Revise	Adopt/ Implement	Monitor	Monitor	Monitor	Monitor/ Plan

Textbook Adoption Plan

Subject	Year 1	Year 2	Year 3	Year 4	Year 5	Year 6
Math	1 2005	2 2006	3 2007	4 2008	5 2009	6 2010
Science	6	1	2	3	4	5
Health	6	1	2	3	4	5
P.E.	6	1	2	3	4	5
Computer Science	6	1	2	3	4	5
Social Studies	5	6	1	2	3	4
Industrial Tech	5	6	1	2	3	4
Reading	4	5	6	1	2	3
Language Arts	4	5	6	1	2	3
Drama	4	5	6	1	2	3
Business	3	4	5	6	1	2
Library Science	3	4	5	6	1	2
Counseling	2	3	4	5	6	1
Home Economics	2	3	4	5	6	1
Math	**1** **2011**	**2** **2012**	**3** **2013**	**4** **2014**	**5** **2015**	**6** **2016**

Key: Using math as a starting point, calendar years have been connected to the years in the revision cycle (Years 1-6). Numbers in boldface indicate revision/adoption that will occur after the year 2010. The last row shows that the complete cycle will begin again with math in 2011.

Figure 3.8

XYZ School District
Sample Curriculum Revision Team Timeline—Year 1

Phase One – Needs Assessment Planning – Curriculum Council

▪ Review test data, national and state trends, teacher surveys	September
▪ Write curriculum area mission statement, consistent with district mission	October
▪ Identify curriculum area program goals	October

Phase Two – Curriculum Revision – Curriculum Revision Team

Applications sent to schools		September
Deadline to submit applications		October
Committee selection		October
First meeting	▪ Train in curriculum design process ▪ Review mission statement, program goals ▪ Review needs assessment ▪ Determine curriculum strands	November
Second meeting	▪ Refine program strands ▪ Identify mastery items by grade level	December
Third meeting	▪ Refine list of mastery items ▪ Place mastery items on scope-and-sequence chart ▪ Evaluate scope-and-sequence mastery chart ▪ Add objectives as needed to scope and sequence	January
Publisher letter requesting preview texts		January
Fourth meeting	▪ Determine time elements ▪ Refine scope and sequence ▪ Request teacher input on scope and sequence	February
Curriculum presentations in buildings		March
Delivery date for available texts		March
Fifth meeting	▪ Review teacher responses ▪ Finalize scope and sequence ▪ Begin development of curriculum guides	April April
Sixth meeting	▪ Continue development of curriculum guides ▪ Plan for textbook review and analysis	May

Assessment Plan Development

File Name	Content
Figure 3.9	Assessment Philosophy
Figure 3.10	Sample Test Descriptions
Figure 3.11	Testing Overview

Figure 3.9 in this guide contains one example of a district's testing philosophy. There are two examples on the accompanying CD. While the mission statement is the same in both cases, the format and the narrative descriptions vary. The sample test descriptions that follow in Figure 3.10 are referenced in the first example.

Figure 3.10 on the CD provides sample test descriptions for a number of tests administered in a district. These samples illustrate just a few of the tests that might be administered in a district and are not intended to be all-inclusive. In this guide, a single test description is included.

Figure 3.11 is a sample matrix of all the assessments given within a district, with the approximate time of year for each assessment. This is similar to the Overview of District Assessments found in Comprehensive Assessment Plan in Section I, but the matrix contained here is more detailed.

Figure 3.9

TESTING IN XYZ SCHOOL DISTRICT
(Sample 1)

Mission

The mission of the Testing Department is to oversee the administration and scoring of both state-mandated tests and district-selected tests and to report the results in a user-friendly format that can be used to improve both curriculum and instruction.

Why test?

For information on students
- To report progress
- To make decisions
- To guide instruction

For accountability
- Individual schools
- District as a whole
- Specific programs

For program improvement
- Curriculum
- Instruction

Tests administered

Test	Grade Level
ACT	Grades 11, 12
Advanced Placement Tests	Grades 10, 11, 12
Bader Reading and Language Inventory	Grade 2
Cognitive Abilities Test	Grades 3, 6
Iowa Test of Basic Skills	Grades 3, 6
Iowa Test of Educational Development	Grades 8, 12
State Assessments	Grades 4-8, 10, 11
Mathematics District Assessments	Grades 3-8
Reading District Assessments	Grades 3-8
Performance Assessments	Grades 3-11
PSAT	Grades 10, 11
SAT	Grades 11, 12

Test Descriptions

A full description of the above tests is on the pages that follow.

Figure 3.10

SAMPLE TEST DESCRIPTIONS
STATE ASSESSMENTS

State assessments are administered yearly at all designated levels in mathematics and reading. Writing has been administered in alternate years, but will now be required yearly at grade 5.

Mathematics: The Mathematics Assessment is administered at Grades 3-8 and 10. The test consists of six multiple-mark items, which can have more than one correct answer and 30 objective items in a single-correct-answer, multiple-choice format. Three process scores and a total mathematical power score are reported for the State Mathematics Assessment. These measures include the following:

- Problem Solving – Problem Solving includes routine and nonroutine problems with relevant and authentic situations, where there is an absence of an apparent or automatic solution strategy. The emphasis is on utilization or problem solving strategies or one's approach to a solution. The score is reported as percent correct.
- Reasoning – Reasoning is the facility to incorporate selective judgment into a solution. Such mathematical problems require the student to make an inference from what is presented and to integrate basic mathematical understandings when producing a solution. The score is reported as percent correct.
- Communication – Communication is the integration of information from other fields than can be approached, understood, or presented mathematically. It involves the skills needed to interpret, express, or form quantitative conclusions that are shared with others. The score is reported as percent correct.
- Mathematical Power – A composite or total score is arrived at by averaging scores from the Problem Solving, Reasoning, and Communication subscales.

Reading: The Reading Assessment is administered at grades 3-8 and 10. The test consists of two extended reading comprehension passages, one narrative, and one expository. Passages are followed by a number of multiple-mark items, which can have more than one correct answer.

- Narrative Text – These selections may include adventure stories; they frequently consist of characters, goals, attempts, and outcomes. The score is reported as percent correct.
- Expository Text – These passages are more informational and have sequential and comparative organizational structures. The score is reported as percent correct.
- Reading Index - A composite or total score is arrived at by averaging scores from the Narrative and Expository selections.

Writing: State Writing Assessments are given at grades 5, 8, and 11. Students are given a choice of prompts on which they can write. Writing samples are scored twice—once by the classroom teacher and then by another teacher trained in the six-trait analytical scoring model. Writing samples are scored on Ideas/Content, Organization, Voice, Word Choice, Sentence Fluency, and Conventions.

TESTING OVERVIEW
XYZ School District

Grade	DISTRICT Math	DISTRICT Reading	STATE ASSESSMENT Reading	STATE ASSESSMENT Math	STATE ASSESSMENT Science	STATE ASSESSMENT Soc. St.	STATE ASSESSMENT Writing	NORM-REFERENCED CogAT	NORM-REFERENCED ITBS	NORM-REFERENCED ITED	PERFORMANCE Math	PERFORMANCE Reading	PERFORMANCE Science	PERFORMANCE Soc. St.	COLLEGE BOARDS PSAT	COLLEGE BOARDS SAT	COLLEGE BOARDS ACT
K																	
1	Qtr. 1-4		Qtr. 1														
2	Qtr. 1-4	Qtr. 1-4	Qtr. 3	Qtr. 3													
3	Qtr. 1-4	Qtr. 1-4	Qtr. 3	Qtr. 3	Qtr. 3			Oct.	April		Sem. 2	Sem. 2[a]	Sem. 2				
4	Qtr. 1-4	Qtr. 1-4	Qtr. 3	Qtr. 3		Qtr. 3	Qtr. 3										
5	Qtr. 1-4	Qtr. 1-4	Qtr. 3	Qtr. 3	Qtr. 3			Oct.	April								
6	Qtr. 1-4	Qtr. 1-4	Qtr. 3	Qtr. 3		Qtr. 3							Sem. 2	Sem. 2			
7	Qtr. 1-4	Qtr. 1-4	Qtr. 3	Qtr. 3	Qtr. 3						Sem. 2	Sem. 2	Sem. 2	Sem. 2			
8	Qtr. 1-4	Qtr. 1-4	Qtr. 3	Qtr. 3		Qtr. 3	Qtr. 3			April							
9																	
10			Qtr. 3	Qtr. 3	Qtr. 3						Sem. 2	Sem. 2	Sem. 2		Fall		
11				Qtr. 3		Qtr. 3	Qtr. 3							Sem. 2	Fall		
12										Fall							

NOTE: Specific dates for assessments are established at the beginning of each school year.

GRADUATION REQUIREMENTS

In addition to completing 23 units, with 12.5 units in specified content areas, students are required to demonstrate competency in the following areas before graduating from any XYZ high school.

    Computer Skills
    Mathematics
    Reading
    Writing

Competency in mathematics and reading is tied to ITED scores, and competency in writing is based on the state assessment (six-trait writing). Computer competency is determined in required computer courses.

Figure 3.11

Scope and Sequence

Figure 3.12 in this guide is a sample application form with a generic job description for curriculum revision work. Materials in Figure 3.12 on the CD include this form as well as letters that can be used to advise principals and teachers of the process and to invite applications and recommendations for team members.

Figure 3.13 contains sample training materials that can be used early in the training of the team that will develop the scope-and-sequence document. Materials on the CD are more extensive than those in this book.

Figure 3.14 provides an example of the analysis involved in deconstructing test items for the purpose of determining the content, context, and cognitive type that apply to a given test item. Two examples are provided on the CD.

Figure 3.15 is an abbreviated scope-and-sequence matrix for K-5 science. State standards on which this sample is based include Process Skills, Life Science, Physical Science, and Earth Science. The sample in the text includes just process skills, while the more extended illustration on the CD includes selected objectives from each standard to illustrate the process of vertical articulation.

Figure 3.16 summarizes a description of Bloom's Taxonomy followed by samples of classification for specific objectives. Materials on the CD are more extensive, with an activity for teachers to complete, and a "key" for the teacher activity.

Figure 3.17 provides an introductory activity that illustrates the need for determining feasibility of a set of curriculum objectives before adoption and implementation. A process for determining time requirements for curriculum objectives written or selected by a writing team is also included. Do the objectives require more time than what has been allocated for the teaching of the subject? On the CD this process is illustrated with a sample format for a single course at one grade level. The two columns provide for initial analysis and then for a revision of time allocations. It may well be that, between the two analyses, some objectives will have been eliminated.

Figure 3.18 is a sample form that can be used to solicit feedback from teachers across the district relative to the proposed scope and sequence.

Figure 3.12

XYZ School District
CURRICULUM COMMITTEE APPLICATION

Applicant's Name _____

Teaching Assignment _____

School _____

Grade Level/Content Area _____

Basic curriculum committee job description:
1. Discuss program goals and develop a mission statement to reflect those goals.
2. Develop grade level/course outcomes.
3. Write specific curriculum objectives.
4. Align specific objectives to national and state standards, the state social studies assessment, and norm-referenced tests.
5. Develop an evaluation component.
6. Select instructional materials.

Committee Selection Process:
- Completed applications must be submitted to Dr. Beverly Greene at the XYZ curriculum office by May 13.
- Applications will be screened and selections will be made by May 20.

Please respond to the following questions in the space provided:

1. Why do you want to be part of the revision committee?

2. What experience do you have in curriculum development?

Teacher signature _____

I support _____ in his/her application for the _____ social studies curriculum development committee member.

Principal signature _____

Figure 3.13

XYZ School District
Foundations of Scope and Sequence Development

Mission

A clear, concise statement telling why the program exists and for whom. It should state a purpose and be idealistic and outcomes-driven.

- *The mission of the science program is to . . .*

Goals

The guiding framework for student performance in the program.

- *Develop mathematical problem solvers.*

Strands

A means to provide organization of the curriculum. Strands may show knowledge, skills, principles, processes, concepts, or connections.

- *Problem Solving*
- *Communication*
- *Reasoning*
- *Inquiry*
- *Technology*
- *Personal and Social Perspectives*

Objectives

Specific learner objectives listed by course or grade.

- *Demonstrate knowledge of types of literature.*

Figure 3.13

XYZ School District
Philosophy of Curriculum Development

100 - 80
Rule

1

Teach 100 Percent of the Adopted Curriculum.

2

The Adopted Curriculum Represents No More Than 80 Percent of the Instructional Days.

Figure 3.14

Sample Test Item Deconstruction Activity

Sample Test Item #1	The grocer placed a sign in front of the display of fresh apples that read "4 apples for $0.79 or 6 for $1." Nancy wanted to buy an apple for each of her lunches for school the next week, but she also wanted a good bargain. What would be her best decision on purchasing the apples? a. 4 apples for $0.79 and one more apple for $0.20 b. 6 apples for $1 with one extra for snacking c. 4 apples for $0.79 and skip the fifth lunch apple d. None of the above
Deconstruction Questions	**Information Derived from Questions**
What is the learning objective being assessed in this item?	*The student will be able to derive accurate information from mathematical calculations and apply them to problem solving in order to make a decision that meets stated requirements.*
What steps or functions must be performed to answer the question?	*The student must calculate the prices per apple according to the information on the sign, then use Nancy's preferences as requirements to guide choice of the "best" decision of those offered as options. The student must think through the "none of the above" option in comparison with the choices to determine clearly that one of the choices meets Nancy's requirements.*
What pre-requisite learning must a student have mastered to answer the question?	*Vocabulary: grocer, display, bargain* *Knowledge of the number of days in the school week (assumed five here)* *Mastery of multiplication and division functions* *Mastery of decimals with reference to dollars and cents* *How to infer meaning from statements that reflect preferences as opposed to clear and definitive facts (e.g., good bargain)*
What cognition types must be employed by the student in answering the question?	*Knowledge of math facts and functions involved, vocabulary* *Comprehension of what is being asked in this problem* *Application of knowledge of math facts and functions to specific problem and information* *Analysis of the steps needed to reach a solution* *Evaluation of the resulting mathematical information in relation to the parameters for choice of the "best response" provided in the problem*

Figure 3.15

Sample Scope and Sequence
Science: PreK-5

Standard #1: Scientific Processes

Topic	PreK	K	1	2	3	4	5
Investigations	**PK.1.1** Compare organisms and objects by their similarities and differences.	**K.1.1** Ask questions about organisms, objects, and events.	**1.1.1** Plan and conduct simple descriptive investigations.	**2.1.1** Plan and conduct simple descriptive investigations based on well-defined questions.	**3.1.1** Plan and implement descriptive investigations that include testable hypotheses.	**4.1.1** Plan and implement descriptive investigations by asking well-defined questions, formulating testable hypotheses, and selecting and using equipment and technology.	**5.1.1** Plan and implement experimental investigations including asking well-defined questions, formulating testable hypotheses, and selecting and using equipment and technology.
Drawing Conclusions	**PK.1.2** Share observations and findings with others through pictures, discussions, or dramatizations.	**K.1.2** Construct reasonable explanations based on observations.	**1.1.2** Construct reasonable explanations and draw conclusions based on observations.	**2.1.2** Construct reasonable explanations and draw conclusions using information and prior knowledge.	**3.1.2** Interpret information to construct reasonable explanations from direct evidence.	**4.1.2** Analyze and interpret information to construct reasonable explanations from direct evidence.	**5.1.2** Analyze and interpret information to construct reasonable explanations from direct and indirect evidence.
Data Collection Tools	**PK.1.3** Use one or more senses to observe and learn about objects, events, and organisms.	**K.1.3** Collect information using tools such as hand lenses, balances, cups, and bowls.	**1.1.3** Collect information using appropriate tools including hand lenses, clocks, thermometers, and balances.	**2.1.3** Collect information using appropriate tools including rulers, meter sticks, measuring cups, clocks, hand lenses, thermometers, and balances.	**3.1.3** Collect and analyze data using appropriate tools including calculators, microscopes, thermometers, hand lenses, meter sticks, rulers, balances, magnets, and compasses.	**4.1.3** Collect and analyze data using appropriate tools including calculators, microscopes, computers, hand lenses, rulers, thermometers, meter sticks, timing devices, balances, magnets, and compasses.	**5.1.3** Collect and analyze data using appropriate tools including calculators, microscopes, cameras, computers, hand lenses, rulers and meter sticks, thermometers, compasses, balances, timing devices, and magnets.

Figure 3.16

XYZ School District
Curriculum Revision
Scope and Sequence Development

Narrative Descriptors of Bloom's Classifications

Cognitive Domain	Definition of Domain	Additional Clarification Comments
Knowledge	Includes those behaviors and test situations that emphasize the remembering, either by recognition or recall, of ideas, material, or phenomena.	Ranges from the specific and relatively concrete types of behaviors to the more complex and abstract ones—including the interrelations and patterns in which information can be organized and structured. Remembering is the major psychological process involved.
Comprehension	When confronted with a written or oral communication, students are expected to know what is being communicated and to be able to make some use of the material or ideas contained in it.	Three types: translation, interpretation, and extrapolation. Emphasis is on the grasp of the meaning and intent of the material.
Application	Apply comprehension in a situation new to the student without prompting, requires transferring of knowledge and comprehension to a real situation.	Emphasis is on the remembering and bringing to bear upon given material the appropriate generalizations or principles.
Analysis	Break down the material into its constituent parts, make explicit the relationships among the elements, and then recognize the organizational principles of the arrangement and structure, which holds together the communication as a whole.	Emphasis is on the breakdown of the material into its constituent parts and detection of the relationship of the parts and of the way they are organized. Not to be confused with comprehending the meaning of something abstract (which is comprehension).
Synthesis	Putting together elements and parts so as to form a whole, to a pattern or structure not clearly there before.	Focus on creative ability of the student but within limits of a framework. Must draw upon elements from many sources and put these together in a structure or pattern not clearly there before. Should yield a product.
Evaluation	Making of judgments about the value, for some purpose, of ideas, works, solution, methods, and material.	Involves use of criteria as well as standards for appraising the extent to which particulars are accurate, effective, economical, or satisfying. May be quantitative or qualitative. Are not opinions but judgments based on criteria.

From Benjamin S. Bloom et al *Taxonomy of Educational Objectives*
Published by Allyn and Bacon, Boston, MA. Copyright © 1984 by Pearson Education
Adapted by permission of the publisher.

Figure 3.16

XYZ School District
Curriculum Revision
Scope and Sequence Development

Bloom's Analysis Activity

Frequently, in analyzing the cognitive domain of a particular learning objective, educators use a list of verbs that is intended to indicate the level of cognition required. Without consideration of the context of these verbs, this practice can lead to serious misclassification. The objectives below, which are all taken from state or local district objectives, are classified using Bloom's narrative descriptions of the cognitive domains. You've been provided with a copy of those descriptions.

Objective	Classification	Comments
Math: Grade 5. Round whole numbers and decimals to any place value.	Knowledge	This requires recall of basic information, with no explanation or restating involved.
Math: Grade 6. Interpret the absolute value of a number as the distance from zero on the number line, and find the absolute value of real numbers.	Comprehension/ knowledge	There are two verbs here. The first, "interpret," would lead one to believe this is at the analysis level. Actually, it is comprehension of the meaning of absolute value. The second verb, "find," requires simple recall of knowledge.
Math: Grade 7. Analyze, interpret, and display data in appropriate bar, line, and circle graphs and stem-and-leaf plots, and justify the choice of display.		There are too many verbs in this objective to really be able to classify it. What are the intended differences between "analyze" and "interpret"? The verb "display" is at a different level than the other verbs. A better objective might be this: Display data in appropriate bar, line, and circle graphs and stem-and-leaf plots, and justify the choice of display. For this objective, "display" is application and "justify" is analysis.
Algebra 1: Solve quadratic equations by using the quadratic formula.	Comprehension	This objective implies exercises in which the student uses the quadratic formula to find a solution. It is practice of a particular skill, but does not move to the application level.

Figure 3.17

What Will You Teach?

You have 12 days left to teach the following objectives. Place an "X" by the ones you will choose to teach in that time.

	Objective	Will Teach
1.	Trace the energy flow through the Krebs cycle and electron transport chain in cellular respiration and in the light and dark reactions in photosynthesis.	_____
2.	Identify and list characteristics of enzymes and explain their role in chemical pathways.	_____
3.	Construct a protein molecule using transcriptions and translation from a DNA molecule.	_____
4.	Illustrate and give an example of sex-linked (X and Y) and incomplete dominance.	_____
5.	Write a pedigree of your family using genetic information.	_____
6.	List some genetic disorders and explain how they are transmitted.	_____
7.	Explain the significance of the voyage of the Beagle and Darwin's visits to the Galapagos Islands and other parts of the world.	_____
8.	Explain the pyramids of energy and biomes and relate them to the process of biological magnification.	_____
9.	Compare nonvascular and vascular plants.	_____
10.	Apply graphing and data analysis skills to interpret scientific data.	_____

Figure 3.17

TIME ANALYSIS

NOTE: Each participant should analyze the objectives for his/her grade level or course. A list of objectives that teachers have written or selected for each course must be prepared before this activity occurs.

Step 1:

Think about the time in terms of hours or minutes you have spent teaching each objective (if the objective is already in your curriculum) or how much time you think it would take you to teach the objective if it is new. Think about mastery—not just coverage.

Don't agonize over this! Give it your best shot in a 5-10 minute period of time.

Add the total number of class periods you have estimated it would take you to teach these curriculum objectives to mastery.

Step 2:

Now look at your assessment report from the most recent state assessment and identify specific trouble areas, based on your own data.

Mark in some way (x,) areas that need more attention (based on the assessment report).

Step 3:

Determine the total amount of time you have available to teach this curriculum. Do you have 60 minutes a day or 90 minutes? Multiply this by the number of days in the school year, but...

Don't forget the 100-80 principle: 100 percent of the curriculum in 80 percent of the time. 80 percent of the time means approximately 150 days (a little less, really, but that makes an easy number to work with). The time available each day should be multiplied by 150, not 180 (the average length of a school year).

Now reconsider your time allocations, keeping two things in mind:

What objectives need more emphasis (based on assessment results)?

What objectives can be eliminated because there is not sufficient time to teach them?

Total your time again, working on the process until you have a reasonable number of objectives that can be taught in the time available.

Step 4:

Once each grade level and each course at the secondary level has completed this process, the entire scope and sequence needs to be revisited. Any time you eliminate an objective along the line you have to consider the impact on future grades or courses.

Share your revised scope and sequence with all teachers who are responsible for teaching this curriculum for review and input. Time is a vital factor in finalizing curricular objectives, but it needs to be done with input from entire faculty—not just the people at this workshop.

Figure 3.18

XYZ School District
Sample Teacher Scope-and-Sequence Curriculum Response Form

Name _____ Building _____

Grade Level / Course _____

1. List the positive things you see in the Mastery Objective Scope Chart:

    _____

    _____

    _____

    _____

    _____

2. List the items you would like to see added or changed:

    _____

    _____

    _____

    _____

    _____

3. Provide any additional comments you want the revision committee to have:

    _____

    _____

    _____

    _____

    _____

Return To: _____ Return Date: _____

Developing Curriculum Guides

Figure 3.19 is a list of tips for writing guides that are both high quality and provide sufficient information to guide teachers in instructional decisions. Any tips provided to writers within a district would need to reflect the specific guide format selected by the district.

Figure 3.20 on the CD provides guide formats for consideration by a district. These formats could be modified to address specific needs or concerns of the district, but each format contains components that will help define and support each objective. A completed sample for a single format appears as Figure 3.20 in this guide.

Figure 3.21 is a sample excerpt showing what a finished curriculum guide might look like. The sample in this book includes a cover page, an acknowledgment page, and a table of contents, while Figure 3.21 on the CD contains those components as well as abbreviated portions of a scope-and-sequence document for K-4 and 5-8, a course description for Grade 6 Mathematics, and the guide pages for one objective from Grade 6 Mathematics. A pacing guide, which is often included in curriculum documents, is not included in this sample. Samples of pacing guides are included in Figure 3.22.

Figure 3.22 in this book contains one sample pacing guide while Figure 3.22 on the CD contains two. Pacing guides are often used in districts where there is high mobility among schools so that teachers from school to school will be in approximately the same place for the majority of students. It should be noted that pacing guides are just that—guides. The needs of students—both individually and collectively—may sometimes override the schedule suggested in the guides.

Figure 3.23 is a partial sample of a completed matrix for evaluating the quality of a curriculum guide, objective by objective. The matrix could be modified to meet district requirements or expectations. A blank matrix is also included on the CD.

Figure 3.19

TIPS FOR WRITING GUIDE PAGES

Include the full language of the stated objective or learning expectation. Use of the verb from the objective in sample assessments and in teaching activities is the key to tight alignment across the written, taught, and tested curriculum.

Text reference: Include the publication date in the first reference to the text. On subsequent guide pages, use just the title and page numbers.

Supplemental resources: List only those resources you will use in relation to the objective. Be specific. If the resource is a video, give the name. If it's a book, list pages.

Time: Give a general estimate of the time required to teach the objective. Example—Three 45-minute periods, or 135 minutes

Teaching activities: Describe (not just list) one or two specific activities you will use related to this objective. If you revisit the objective periodically during the year, say so and give your total teaching time across all those class sessions.

Assessment: Again, provide some specificity. How will you know students have met the objective you are addressing? Include more than one type of response, such as multiple choice, constructed response, teacher observation, or performance assessment.

Make sure your details (your entire guide page) support your topic sentence (the objective at the top of the page).

Figure 3.20

SAMPLE CURRICULUM GUIDE PAGE

K	1	2	3	4	5	6
			I	M		

Objective: Use manipulatives or models to illustrate equivalent fractions.

Vocabulary:
- Numerator
- Denominator
- Equivalent fractions

District References:
- Heath   p. 35-37
- Scott Foresman p. 45-55, 62-63
- Jostens   3AJ36

Optional Resources:
- Fraction circles
- Fraction bars
- Cuisenaire rods

Teaching time:	2 hours
Assessment:	State test
	Teacher's test
Strand:	Number sense
Exit outcome:	#3
Math program goal:	#4
Bloom's type:	Comprehension
Objective code:	MA.3.1.5

Teaching Activities:
- Use fraction circles or Cuisenaire rods to model equivalent fractions.
- Play Fraction War with fraction bars.
- Play Fraction Concentration with fraction bars.

Expansions:
- Write in journal how one can use fraction circles to find an equivalent fraction for 1/2.
- Show equivalence of various coins, such as 5 dimes = 1 half-dollar.
- Add $1/2 + 1/3$ using fraction circles.

Assessment Items:
Performance: Use fraction bars, fraction circles, or Cuisenaire rods to show that $3/6 = 1/2$.

Multiple choice: Which of the following fractions is equivalent to 1/3?
            A. $3/12$ B. $4/12$ C. $3/6$ D. $6/9$

Figure 3.21

**XYZ School District
Curriculum Guide:
Mathematics Grade 6**

September 2005

Curriculum Team Members:

**Joan Jenkins, Mathematics Curriculum Coordinator
Facilitator**

**Tom Jefferson, Lovely Middle School
Ellie Roosevelt, Happy Middle School
Johnny Adams, Friendly Middle School**

*XYZ School District
1202 S. 6th Avenue
Anywhere, U.S. 83982*

George Johnston, Ph.D., Superintendent

Alice Barnwell, Ph.D., Director, Curriculum and Assessment

ACKNOWLEDGMENTS

Development, review, or revision of any curriculum involves numerous individuals and groups in order to produce a quality product that meets teachers' and students' needs and provides alignment of the written, taught, and tested curriculum. The work includes research, data analysis, intensive dialogue, and expert decision making. We hope that this curriculum document reflects the accomplishments of each of those steps and meets the test of quality for serving instructional needs.

During the past year, the following individuals and groups have contributed significantly to production of this curriculum guide. Appreciation of the efforts cannot be overstated!

Teachers on the Curriculum Team
Tom Jefferson, Lovely Middle School
Ellie Roosevelt, Happy Middle School
Johnny Adams, Friendly Middle School

Administrators Who Provided Feedback and Assistance
Jay Bedden, Principal, Lovely Middle School
Alicia Miller, Principal, Happy Middle School
Roy Riddleman, Principal, Friendly Middle School

Teachers Who Provided Feedback and Other Assistance
Ellie Farmer, Lovely Middle School
Sandra Jenkins, Lovely Middle School
Maryanne Mitchell, Lovely Middle School
George Pickel, Happy Middle School
Andy Krieke, Happy Middle School
Candace Therman, Friendly Middle School
Dwight Ingerman, Friendly Middle School

District Staff on the Curriculum Team
Joan Jenkins, Math Curriculum Coordinator (Facilitator)
Dr. Beverly Greene, Director of Curriculum (Revision Coordinator)

A special thanks to the parents who visited the document presentations at all three middle schools and provided the team with meaningful questions and valuable feedback during this review and production process.

Figure 3.21

Figure 3.21

Table of Contents

Figure 3.22

XYZ SCHOOL DISTRICT
PACING GUIDE: ENGLISH LANGUAGE ARTS CURRICULUM
GRADE 7
(Sample page from a pacing guide)

The following information on sequencing of instruction for the delivery of the Grade 7 English Language Arts curriculum is intended to provide an estimated framework for classroom teachers. References to objectives by code match the strand and objective code designations in the district curriculum guides and in the scope and sequence for your curriculum area. Depending on the needs of your students, the pacing may need to be adjusted by one to two weeks over the year. Assistance from curriculum staff should be requested if you are finding it necessary for further changes. Our goal is to help ensure that all students receive access to the intended curriculum during the planned grade level.

Curriculum Objectives (clustered but may be separated if needed)	Estimated Instructional Time Allocation (as estimated in guides)	Planned Month of Implementation
7.1.1, 7.1.2, 7.3.1	4-6 hours	September
7.1.3, 7.3.2	3 hours	September
7.1.4, 7.1.6, 7.1.12	3 hours	September
7.2.1, 7.2.2, 7.2.3	2 hours	September
7.2.4, 7.1.5, 7.2.5, 7.3.3	3 hours	September
7.3.4	2 hours	September
7.3.5, 7.4.1, 7.4.2	3 hours	October
7.1.7, 7.2.5	3 hours	October
7.1.8, 7.2.6, 7.3.5	5 hours	October
7.3.6, 7.3.7, 7.1.9	5-7 hours	October
7.3.8	2 hours	October
7.4.2, 7.4.3	2 hours	October
7.3.9	3 hours	October

Figure 3.23

XYZ School District
Sample Curriculum Guide Analysis

Subject: <u>Math</u>   **Grade:** <u>Kindergarten</u>   **Reviewer:** <u>John Smith</u>

Directions: Write the objective numbers for the grade/course you are reviewing across the top row. You may need to use more than one analysis sheet. Review the guide page for each instructional objective and indicate the presence of alignment in each area.

X = Yes
0 = No
N = Not Applicable

		K 1	K 2	K 3	K 4	K 5	K 6	K 7	K 8	K 9	K 10	K 11	K 12	K 13	K 14	K 15	K 16	K 17
									Objective Number									
Congruence	Teaching activity matches objective	X	O	O	X	O	O	O	O	X	X	X	O	O	O	X	X	X
	Assessment matches objective	X	X	X	X	X	X	X	X	X	X	X	X	X	X	X	X	X
	Bloom's type is accurate	X	O	O	X	X	O	O	O	O	X	O	X	X	O	X	X	O
	Objective matches Bloom's type	X	X	X	X	X	X	X	X	X	X	X	X	X	X	X	X	X
	Teaching activity matches Bloom's type	X	O	O	O	O	O	O	O	O	X	X	O	X	O	O	O	X
Alignment	National standards	X	X	X	X	X	X	X	X	X	X	X	X	X	X	X	X	X
	State standards	X	X	X	X	X	X	X	X	X	X	X	X	X	X	X	X	X
Resources	External assessments: content and format	N	N	N	N	N	N	N	N	N	N	N	N	N	N	N	N	N
	Textbook support	X	X	X	X	O	O	X	X	X	O	O	X	X	X	X	X	O
	Supplementary materials support	O	O	X	X	X	X	X	X	X	O	O	X	X	X	X	X	X
	Variety of resources listed	X	X	X	X	X	X	X	X	X	X	X	X	X	X	X	X	X
Expansions	Real world / job related	X	O	O	O	O	O	O	O	O	O	X	O	O	O	O	O	O
	Integration with other subjects	X	X	X	X	X	X	X	X	X	X	X	X	X	X	O	O	O
	Higher order thinking skills	X	O	O	O	O	X	O	O	O	O	X	O	O	O	O	O	X
	SPED adaptations	X	O	O	O	O	O	O	O	O	O	O	O	O	O	O	O	O
Equity	No gender, race, or cultural bias	X	X	X	X	X	X	X	X	X	X	X	X	X	X	X	X	X
Time	Number of days / lessons	X	X	X	X	X	X	X	X	X	X	X	X	X	X	X	X	X

Materials Selection

File Name	Content
Figure 3.24	Principal and Teacher Communication about Review Process
Figure 3.25	Timelines for Materials Selection
Figure 3.26	Letters to Textbook Companies; Interview Questions
Figure 3.27	Initial Review of Texts; Deep Alignment Analysis; Review Summaries
Figure 3.28	Information about Piloting
Figure 3.29	Samples of Materials Evaluation Summaries after Piloting

Figure 3.24 contains memos and letters relative to the materials review process. This book contains a single letter, while the CD contains two examples.

Figure 3.25 provides examples of timelines that could be used in the materials selection process.

Figure 3.26 in this book contains an initial letter to a textbook representative, a completed form for requesting sample materials, and a list of questions that can be used in the interview process to ensure that the same questions are asked of all publisher representatives. This same file on the CD contains additional examples.

Figure 3.27 contains an abbreviated sample of a completed textbook review and evaluation. The CD contains additional examples of ways that textbooks can be reviewed. Some examples are based on deep alignment analysis that addresses how specific district objectives are covered in the materials being reviewed and the kind of assessment alternatives that are included for teachers.

Figure 3.28 provides examples relative to piloting if a district chooses to pilot materials before adoption. The CD file is more extensive than the single example that appears here.

Figure 3.29 documents (abbreviated here, more illustrative on the CD) are examples of summaries that can be put together by a school district in the textbook review process.

Figure 3.24

XYZ SCHOOL DISTRICT
MEMORANDUM
(Sample memo to revision team regarding materials selection committee)

To: Curriculum Revision Team – Language Arts
From: Dr. Beverly Greene
Re: Team Members for Materials Selection Committee – Language Arts K-12
Date: _____

As we discussed in our recent team meeting, the Curriculum Department will be choosing committee members for the selection of Instructional Materials for the K-12 Language Arts curriculum this month. The purpose of this memorandum is to invite those of you who are interested in working on the selection of language arts textbooks and "core" materials for the next cycle to indicate your interest by sending me an e-mail message to that effect by Wednesday, _____.

It is the intent to have half of the 14 members from the Curriculum Revision Team in order to assist in communicating any ideas, problems, or needs that surfaced during the curriculum revision work that need to be considered as materials are reviewed. The other members will be chosen from the applicants from all grade levels. When we have both groups' interests known, the Assistant Superintendent and I will review the candidates' experience and designate a team to represent the K-12 practitioners to work on the committee. We anticipate that decision by Friday, _____.

Committee members will be paid the stipends outlined for this work in the bargained agreement.

Please assist us by encouraging your colleagues to express their interests and join us in this important task for effectively implementing the revised curriculum.

Thanks again for your service and excellent work on the curriculum revision.

Figure 3.25

XYZ School District
Curriculum Revision
Materials Selection Process and Timeline

Possible Timeline	Activity	Responsibility
Summer	Identify available instructional materials/textbooks	_____
Summer	Conduct team evaluation of materials	_____
Summer	Interview publisher/vendor finalists	_____
Summer	Select materials for expanded review	_____
Oct.-Dec.	Provide preview period for staff	_____
December	Collect preview response forms	_____
January	Hold publisher presentations in district	_____
January	Collect post-presentation response forms	_____
February	Review all information in team	_____
February	Choose materials for recommended purchase	_____
February	Give recommendation to Superintendent and Board for approval	_____
March	Order materials	_____
March	Designate team for follow-up work on supplemental materials as needed	_____
May	Receive materials in district, distribute to buildings	_____
June or August	Provide initial staff development	_____
August-May	Provide continuous debriefing and support during implementation	_____

Figure 3.25

XYZ School District
Curriculum Revision
Materials Selection Process and Timeline

NOTE: Below is a generic textbook publishers' meeting agenda for those publishers that have been invited to meet with school district personnel regarding a textbook selection timeline.

Action	Deadline
Publisher Commitment to Proceed	August
Preview Materials Needed	August
Preview materials	
Pilot materials	
Preview Materials to the District	September
Materials reviewed by teachers	
Pilot materials used by students	
Publisher Interview with School Personnel	November
Cost of materials	
Fixed pricing	
Support materials included	
Staff development support	
Timeliness of delivery	
Shipping rates	
Correlation with state indicators	
Publisher Presentations in School District	January
District Selection of Materials	February
Preview teacher survey data	
Principal survey data	
Pilot teacher survey data	
Instructional department review	
Support in Ordering Materials	March
Delivery of Materials	June
Teacher additions and resources	
Student materials	

Figure 3.26

XYZ SCHOOL DISTRICT
300 Pine Street
Anyplace, USA
(Sample initial letter to textbook publishers)

Date

John Smith, Representative
High Performance Publishing Company
1500 High Drive
Zanetown, U.S.A.

Dear Mr. Smith:

The XYZ School District will be purchasing new texts this spring in secondary social studies. Texts will be purchased for the following courses: American History, American History AP, U.S. Government, U.S. Government AP, Psychology 1, Psychology 2, and Psychology AP.

After reviewing the materials provided by your company, our revision committee has decided to further examine the following materials from your company:

America Pathways to Present

Introduction to Psychology
Understanding Psychology
Arthur's American Government

A list of schools, addresses, and needed materials is attached to this letter. We would appreciate your help in sending these materials to the schools listed above by February 1. We will do our reviews of the materials during February and March. Selections and ordering will take place in April.

Please include textual materials with the latest copyright date. If the text is to be updated during this school year, please inform us. All contacts concerning the pilot project should be addressed to Mr. Bill Jones. We ask that you not make personal contacts with the piloting teachers during the school day.

Thank you for your interest in this project.

Sincerely,

Preview Materials Request Form (included with above letter)

Text	Materials Needed	School	Contact
America Pathways to Present	TE or preview kit	South	Bill Jones

Figure 3.26

XYZ School District
Curriculum Revision
Textbook Selection Process

Sample Materials Needed from Publishers

Elementary

Material Type	Quantity	Grade Level	Contents
Sampler Set	22 sets	K-6	1 student text 1 teacher's edition 1 resource kit
Classroom Set	2 sets	K-6	30 student texts 1 teacher's edition 1 resource kit

Middle School

Material Type	Quantity	Grade Level	Contents
Sampler Set	7 sets	7-8	1 student text 1 teacher's edition 1 resource kit
Classroom Set	2 sets	7-8	30 student texts 1 teacher's edition 1 resource kit

High School

Material Type	Quantity	Grade Level	Contents
Sampler Set	5 sets	9-12	1 student text 2 teacher's editions 1 resource kit
Classroom Set	2 sets	9-12	30 student texts 1 teacher's edition 1 resource kit

Figure 3.26

XYZ School District
Curriculum Revision
Materials Selection Process

Publisher/Vendor Interviews

Publisher_____ Date _____ Interviewer _____

Pricing   **3   2   1**

What is the cost of the text?

Are there any quantity price breaks? What are those?

Will you be able to establish a fixed price for the text? For how long?

Materials   **3   2   1**

What supplemental materials are included with the purchase?

How long will the materials be available through your warehouse?

Can you add a bar code label to each book?

Can we have permission to copy audiocassettes? CDs?

How do you want the pilot/preview materials returned to you?

Will you provide copies of alignment correlations of the text with state standards and assessments?

Staff Development   **3   2   1**

What will be the level of support provided for staff development?

Shipping   **3   2   1**

What will the shipping rates be?

Will you guarantee a delivery date?

Can you ship everything to one site, labeled by each school?

Figure 3.27

XYZ School District
Curriculum Revision
Materials Selection Process

Resource Evaluation (Example B)

Subject/Grade Level __Math 6__   Textbook/Resource __Text A__   Evaluator __Ima Winner__

Directions: Use the rating scale at the bottom of the page to indicate how each textbook or major resource being reviewed supports the learning objectives for the course. Include specific page correlations that can later be used in curriculum guides. The index can help you locate topics, but be sure to review thoroughly ways in which the topic is taught and assessed. Does the textbook's coverage meet district objectives?

Learning Objective	Resource Alignment Rating	Assessment Alignment Rating	Page correlations Gaps, with Suggestions for Supplements
Explain the relationship among decimals, fractions, and percents.	3	1	Chapter 10—Section 1, plus pp. 434, 470, 488 Assessment—only short answer, constructed response; no multiple choice, like state assessment
Convert percents to decimals and fractions and terminating decimals to fractions or percents.	3	2	Chapter 10 (entire chapter), plus pp. 434-436, 471, 489 Assessment—short answer, skills used in performance assessments; no multiple choice.
Find a given percent of any number.	2	2	Chapter 10-Section 3, plus pp. 434-436, 472, 504 (Tool Box at end of book) Assessment—short answer, skills used in performance assessments; no multiple choice (like state)

Rubric for Rating Resource Alignment	
3 Strong	Clearly addresses all elements of the objective; offers many opportunities to learn objective; good support materials for teaching
2 Adequate	Objective is addressed with practice opportunities; adequate teaching ideas
1 Weak	Objective is minimally addressed with limited teaching ideas; some supplement needed
0 Missing	Objective is missing from materials; needs complete supplement

Rubric for Rating Assessment Alignment	
3 Strong	Several assessment approaches included
2 Adequate	More than one assessment method included
1 Weak	One assessment method suggested
0 Missing	No assessment method included

Figure 3.28

XYZ SCHOOL DISTRICT
MEMORANDUM
(Letter to solicit pilot teachers)

To: K-5 Classroom Teachers
    Middle School English/Language Arts Teachers
    High School English/Language Arts Teachers

From: Dr. Beverly Greene

Re: Volunteers for Piloting of Instructional Materials – Language Arts K-12

Date: _____

Thanks to the dedicated work of your Curriculum Revision Team and the Instructional Materials Selection Committee, we are now ready to pilot the top two choices of materials at each level before making a final recommendation to the Superintendent and Board for purchase of the core materials for the next cycle.

So many of you have participated in revision, materials selection, and feedback work that we are hoping your interest in piloting use of materials might be high as well. The committee has suggested that we pilot use of materials from the top two publishing sources. They also have suggested that we need not pilot all levels, but that we should pilot at least alternating grade levels with feedback opportunities for all at predetermined points in the nine-weeks piloting period. My department has concurred with these recommendations.

Four members from the Curriculum Revision Team and the Instructional Materials Selection Committee will be helping the Assistant Superintendent and me choose teachers for piloting of the materials. Ideally, we would like to have two teachers from each grade level pilot materials so that comparative experiences can be discussed with the committee before final recommendations are determined.

Teachers who volunteer to pilot materials will have six to eight after-school materials/curriculum implementation meetings and will be paid for that time at the contracted stipend rate; they will also receive the "special assignment" bonus in accordance with the bargained contract.

Teachers interested in piloting the materials should indicate that interest to me by e-mail no later than the end of the school day on Tuesday, _____. Include your grade level or course, school, and years teaching that grade level or course.

We expect to make the selection of teachers to pilot by the middle of the following week. We hope you will seriously consider this contribution to the selection of materials that you will all be using for the next cycle.

Figure 3.29

XYZ School District
Sample Forms for Summary of Evaluations by Groups

The textbook series receiving the most #1 and #2 rankings are included; the percentages of teachers ranking the material as #1 or #2 are listed.

Group	Rated First Choice	Rated Second Choice
Grades K-1	*e.g., Company C (80%)*	*e.g., Company D (62%)*
Grades 2-3		
Grades 4-5		
Grades 6-8 Eng./LA Teachers		
9-12 English Teachers		
Pilot Teachers Only		
Curriculum Specialists and District Administrators		
Principals/Asst. Principals		

Pilot Teacher Preference	Average Ranking	Percent of Teachers Ranking as #1	Percent of Teachers Ranking as #2
Company A	1.6		
Company B	2.2		
Company C	3.5		
Company D	3.9		

Non-Pilot Teacher Preference	Average Ranking	Percent of Teachers Ranking as #1	Percent of Teachers Ranking as #2
Company A	1.8		
Company B	2.1		
Company C	3.0		
Company D	3.6		

Principal Preference	Average Ranking	Percent of Principals Ranking as #1	Percent of Principals Ranking as #2
Company A	1.1		
Company B	3.1		
Company C	2.8		
Company D	4.2		

Assessment Design

File Name	Content
Figure 3.30	Timeline for Assessment Development Process
Figure 3.31	Sample Planning Guide for Instruction and Assessment
Figure 3.32	Test Specifications for One Quarterly Test

Figure 3.30 contains a timeline for development of local assessments in a given content area. Development of the information outlined in Figures 3.31 and 3.32 below will support the overall timeline for development of local assessments.

Figure 3.31 is a combination pacing and assessment plan. It indicates which objectives will be taught in each quarter, including those that will be taught in multiple quarters. It also indicates those objectives that will be tested each quarter, including the "ramping up" of assessments for those skills that build across the years. Because this is at the kindergarten level, most assessments would be performance assessments with mastery determined by teacher observation.

Figure 3.32 models the development of test specifications for a specific test at a specific grade level.

Figure 3.30

XYZ School District
Assessment Development Timeline

Activity	Timeline
Finalize scope and sequence.	_____
Select assessment writing team.	_____
Establish assessment parameters (grade levels, number of tests).	_____
Provide initial training in fundamentals of assessment.	_____
Identify objectives to be tested at each grade level or course.*	_____
Create a matrix for each assessment with objectives, number of items per objective, and method of assessment.	_____
Provide additional training in writing specific types of assessments at different cognitive levels.	_____

Write assessments.*

	Test 1	_____
	Test 2	_____
	Test 3	_____
	Test 4	_____

Review and edit assessments; prepare answer keys.*

	Test 1	_____
	Test 2	_____
	Test 3	_____
	Test 4	_____

Produce and disseminate assessments.*

	Test 1	_____
	Test 2	_____
	Test 3	_____
	Test 4	_____

*The number of assessments depends upon the testing parameters established.

Figure 3.31

MATHEMATICS OBJECTIVES
KINDERGARTEN
Year-Long Planning Guide for Instruction and Assessment

Kindergarten Standards and Objectives	Qtr. 1	Qtr. 2	Qtr. 3	Qtr. 4
Number Sense				
Demonstrate one-to-one correspondence by matching sets of objects one-to-one up to 10 objects.	A			
Count, recognize, represent, name, and order a number of objects (up to 10).	count/ recognize **A**	represent/ order **A**	write **A**	
Count to 100 by ones and tens.				A
Find the number that is one more than or one less than any whole number up to 10.				A
Use correctly the words none/some/all, more/less, most/least, and before/after (the latter in relationship to a line of numbers up to 10).				
Divide sets of objects (even numbers up to 10) into two equal parts.				A
Divide shapes into two equal parts.				
Computation				
Model addition by joining sets of objects (for any two sets with fewer than 10 objects when joined).			A	
Model subtraction by removing objects from sets (for numbers less than 10).			A (with addition)	
Describe addition and subtraction situations (for numbers less than 10).				
Algebra and Functions				
Recognize and extend simple patterns with numbers and shapes.	A	A	A	
Geometry				
Identify and describe common geometric objects, including circle, triangle, square, rectangle, and cube.		A		
Compare and sort common objects by position, shape, and size.		A		
Identify and use terms of spatial relationships: inside, outside, between, above, and below.				
Identify geometric shapes and structures in the environment including circle, square, rectangle, and triangle.	A			

Figure 3.32

Test Specifications
Grade 3 Mathematics—Test 1

Problem #	Objective	Descriptor	# of Items
1, 2, 3, 4, 5, 6, 30*	**3.2.1**	**Add/subtract whole numbers**	**7**
7, 8, 18	**3.2.5**	**Multiplication facts (2, 5, 10)**	**3**
9	3.1.7	Odd/even	1
10, 11	3.1.3	Represent numbers	2
12, 28*	3.1.2	Place value	2
13	3.1.5	Compare and arrange	1
14	3.1.1	Count, read, write numbers	1
15	3.1.4	Identify numbers from different combinations	1
16	3.2.7	Estimation	1
17, 21, 22, 29*	3.3.3	Operation symbols	4
19, 20	3.5.10b	Write money amounts	2
24	3.4.5	Congruent figures	1
23	3.4.7	Line segments and lines	1
25	3.4.8	Lines of symmetry	1
26, 27	3.5.9a	Time intervals and duration	2
		Total	30
		Computation	**10**

*Items marked with an asterisk are application problems that require a constructed response. Other items are multiple choice. Constructed response problems test problem solving as well as specific content.
Bold-faced items indicate computation problems.

Staff Development and Implementation

File Name **Content**
Figure 3.33   Sample Staff Development Calendar
Figure 3.34   Sample Parent Brochure

Figure 3.33 is a sample calendar for staff development across the greater part of a school year for the content area under revision—in this case, English Language Arts.

Figure 3.34 provides an example of a brochure that can be developed to inform parents about what their children will be learning in a specific grade. The important part of this example is not the cover page; rather, it is the content contained in the columns under each subject heading. Statements regarding what students will learn should be simplified to avoid any jargon. Learning objectives for library skills, fine arts, and physical education can be easily included. This brochure can be provided on the district's Web site as well as in hard copy.

Suggestions for supporting ongoing implementation are contained in the section on Monitoring.

Figure 3.33

XYZ SCHOOL DISTRICT
STAFF DEVELOPMENT CALENDAR OF DISTRICT OFFERINGS
(sample pages)

Note: The calendar includes the Professional Development Academy in August as well as other days for which partial stipends will be provided by the Learning for Winning Grant funds for those teachers who attend.

R=Required of all teachers teaching in this curriculum (professional development pay by district if non-contracted day)
RW=Required attendance; contracted working day
O=Optional; recommended for teachers new to district and/or specific practice addressed; partial stipends provided by grant

Staff Development for Curriculum, Instruction, and Assessment
Fall 2004 through Summer 2006
(sample pages from calendar)

Dates	New Curriculum and Materials	Instructional Strategies and Student Work Alignment	Assessment Planning, Writing, Interpretation and Use of Data Reports	Related Training for School and District Administrators
August 23-24	English Language Arts Curriculum (K-5) (R)			
August 23-24		Active & Experiential Teaching for High School Courses in English Language Arts (O)		
August 25-26	English Language Arts (6-8) (R)	Using new textbooks for ELA K-5 (R)	(with teachers for Day 1; Day 2 = Administrators session)	(with ELA teachers for Day 1 of curriculum; Day 2 = Administrators)

Figure 3.34

SECOND GRADE CURRICULUM

Mathematics
Language Arts
Science
Social Studies

Sunflower School District
1000 Sunflower Way
City, State, Zip

Web address

Figure 3.34

Grade 2 Mathematics

Read and write numbers through 999.

Order and compare numbers through 999 using numbers and the symbols for greater than, less than, and equal.

Recall and apply basic addition and subtraction facts (sums to 18).

Solve addition or subtraction problems using two-digit numbers, with and without regrouping.

Learn and apply multiplication facts 0, 1, 2, 3, 4, 5, 10, and 100.

Identify and write fractional parts of a whole object (not to exceed twelfths) when given a concrete representation.

Determine the value of a collection of coins less than one dollar.

Identify, describe, and extend numeric and geometric patterns.

Identify attributes of any two-dimensional or three-dimensional figure.

Use whole numbers to locate and name points on a line.

Measure length to the nearest inch and half inch and weight to the nearest pound.

Read a thermometer.

Read time on a clock to the nearest five minutes.

Construct picture graphs and bar graphs.

Answer questions based on picture graphs and bar graphs.

Select and use an appropriate problem-solving strategy (drawing a picture, looking for a pattern, systematic guessing and checking, or acting it out) to solve a problem.

Grade 2 Reading

Retell or act out the important events in stories using a variety of graphic organizers.

Blend initial letter-sounds with common vowel spelling patterns to read words.

Decode by using all letter-sound correspondences within a word.

Recognize high frequency irregular words such as said, was, where, and is.

Read both regular and irregular words automatically

Use structural cues such as prefixes and suffixes to recognize words, for example, un- and –ly.

Use knowledge of word order (syntax) and context to support word identification and confirm word meaning.

Recognize character traits: thoughts, feelings, relationships, and changes.

Restate the story problem(s) or plot using visuals and graphic organizers.

Describe the importance of the setting to a story's meaning by using visuals such as graphic organizers.

Explain how the author's perspective or point of view affects the text.

Find examples of different forms of texts, including newsletters, poems, narratives, and informative texts.

Make and explain inferences from texts such as determining important ideas, causes and effects, making predictions, and drawing conclusions.

Distinguish fiction from nonfiction, including fact and fantasy.

Identify conclusions with examples drawn from text.

Figure 3.34

Grade 2 Science

Demonstrate safe practices during classroom and field investigations.

Plan and conduct simple descriptive investigations.

Construct and communicate reasonable explanations about investigations.

Communicate explanations about investigations.

Identify characteristics of living organisms.

Describe differences between living and nonliving things.

Compare and give examples of the ways living organisms depend on each other and on their environments.

Identify organisms with similar needs, such as oxygen, water, food, or space.

Give examples of some inherited traits of plants and animals.

Describe the functions of plant parts (roots, stems, leaves).

Identify and give examples of different forms of matter (liquids, solids, and gases).

Describe and give examples of how heat causes change in different forms of matter, such as melting and evaporation.

Describe changes in weather, including measuring and recording temperature changes.

Describe changes in seasons.

Describe and interpret steps of the water cycle.

Identify and describe (orally and or in writing) properties of soil.

Grade 2 Social Studies

Explain the significance of various community, state, and national celebrations such as Memorial Day, Independence Day, Veterans' Day, and Thanksgiving.

Use appropriate vocabulary related to chronology of events, including past, present, and future.

Use symbols to find locations and determine primary directions (east, west, north, south) on maps and globes.

Identify major landforms and bodies of water, including continents and oceans, on maps and globes.

Locate your community, your state, the United States, and Canada and Mexico on maps and globes.

Describe ways in which people depend on the physical environment, including natural resources, to meet basic needs.

Distinguish between a producer and a consumer.

Give examples of how science and technology have changed communication, transportation, and recreation.

Identify responsibilities of governments and describe how those actions help us.

Compare ways that public officials are selected, including election and appointment to office.

Obtain information about a topic using print sources such as pictures, magazines, textbooks, and encyclopedias.

Obtain information from electronic sources, such as films, television, and the Internet.

Monitoring

File Name	Content
Figure 3.35	Sample Monitoring Plan
Figure 3.36	Teacher's Planning Guide
Figure 3.37	Curriculum/Textbook Feedback Form (Teachers)
Figure 3.38	Linkage of Student Work to Standards & Objectives (Teachers)
Figure 3.39	Linkage of Student Work to Standards & Objectives (Principals)

Figure 3.35 is an outline of a complete monitoring process that includes both district and building personnel.

Figure 3.36 is a sample of a format that can be used for teacher planning. If a pacing guide or teaching sequence is in place for the district, this form would not be used. Note that the format and content are the same as those used in Figure 3.31. The same planning documents can be used in multiple places, avoiding duplication of efforts. Storing documents electronically in a specific location that has been reserved for staff members working on curriculum and assessment will enable those individuals to retrieve documents and incorporate them as necessary into other processes when appropriate.

Also note that teachers' plans should match those contained in any district plan used for district-wide assessments, such as that contained in Figure 3.31. In fact, the latter can virtually become the *de facto* planning guide for teachers.

Figure 3.37 provides a mechanism for teachers to submit specific feedback, especially during the first year of curriculum implementation or use of new materials.

Figure 3.38 guides teachers in self-analysis of the materials they are using to teach a particular objective. The goal of the analysis is to strengthen the match between materials being used and the objective students are being expected to master. The worksheet provides for the analysis of a single artifact.

Figure 3.39 is a similar analysis of linkage between student work and curricular objectives that principals might use. The printed example has been completed, while the CD also contains a blank template that can be modified to meet the needs of individual users. Principals could also use Figure 3.38, but Figure 3.39 provides for analysis of multiple artifacts on the same page.

Figure 3.35

XYZ SCHOOL DISTRICT

CURRICULUM MONITORING PROCESS
A Team Approach with Shared Responsibilities

DISTRICT

Curriculum staff visits school-based team meetings (grade level teams, vertical meetings with specific curriculum topics on agendas, secondary course teams, or department meetings). (Three times per team per year or as needed)

Curriculum staff visits classrooms for first-hand understanding of implementation and support to teachers as needed. (Twice per semester or as needed)

Principal supervisor visits meetings and classrooms occasionally with principal or assistant principal. (Once or twice per semester or as needed)

Curriculum staff arranges logistics for grade-level or clustered-levels meetings across schools for progress review and implementation support as needed. (Once per semester or as needed)

SCHOOL

Principals (and assistant principals) visit classrooms regularly and informally to become familiar with curriculum implementation and support teachers as needs are identified. (Once weekly)

Individual teachers record notes on their concerns or successes with curriculum objectives or instructional materials. (Ongoing)

Teachers meet in grade level teams or vertical curricular groups to share progress with curriculum implementation (pacing checks, materials, activities, curriculum objectives, and assessments). (Once monthly or every six weeks)

Note: Times and frequency of meetings are suggestions and may be adapted according to need.

Figure 3.36

KINDERGARTEN MATHEMATICS OBJECTIVES
YEAR-LONG PLANNING GUIDE

Kindergarten Standards and Objectives	Qtr. 1	Qtr. 2	Qtr. 3	Qtr. 4
Number Sense				
Demonstrate one-to-one correspondence by matching sets of objects one-to-one up to 10 objects.				
Count, recognize, represent, name, and order a number of objects (up to 10).				
Count to 100 by ones and tens.				
Find the number that is one more than or one less than any whole number up to 10.				
Use correctly the words one/many, none/some/all, more/less, most/least, and before/after (the latter in relationship to a line of numbers up to 10).				
Divide sets of 10 or fewer into equal parts.				
Divide shapes into equal parts.				
Computation				
Model addition by joining sets of objects (for any two sets with fewer than 10 objects when joined).				
Model subtraction by removing objects from sets (for numbers less than 10).				
Describe addition and subtraction situations (for numbers less than 10).				
Algebra and Functions				
Recognize and extend simple patterns with numbers and shapes.				
Geometry				
Identify and describe common geometric objects, including circle, triangle, square, rectangle, and cube.				
Compare and sort common objects by position, shape, and size.				
Identify and use terms of spatial relationships: inside, outside, between, above, and below.				
Identify geometric shapes and structures in the environment, including circle, square, rectangle, and triangle.				

Figure 3.37

XYZ SCHOOL DISTRICT
TEACHER NOTES FOR FORMATIVE FEEDBACK

Curriculum Area _____   **Teacher** _____

Grade Level/Course _____   **School** _____

The purpose of this form is to provide a systematic way for teachers to record concerns, successes, or other types of feedback for use in team monitoring discussions and the curriculum review process. Teachers may submit copies periodically to the curriculum office as they use the notes in monitoring discussions, or they may collect the notes and submit them as review begins. (Note: Any district using this form would need to provide specific instructions in this space.)

Objective	Materials in Use	Feedback Notes

Figure 3.38

XYZ SCHOOL DISTRICT
Checking Linkage of Student Work to Standards and Curriculum Objectives: A Teacher's Worksheet

The purpose of this form is to help teachers and principals review the parallelism between curriculum standards and student learning objectives being taught and tested and the student work assignments in use. The intent is to promote tight congruence from objective to performance and then to assessments in order to enhance student capacity to demonstrate mastery of intended knowledge and skills.

Description of Sample of Student Work (Artifact), including instructions provided:

_____

_____

_____

Curriculum Area/Course: _____

Standard: _____

Objective: _____

Item	Content	Context	Cognitive Type	Curriculum Grade Level	Grade Level of Sample
Standard					
Objective					
Work Sample					
Comments					

Figure 3.39

Analysis Sheet: Student Work Samples

School: Happy Valley Elementary   Date: March 4, 2005   Evaluator: Ima Principal

Grade/Subject	Sample #	Description of Work Sample	Objective(s) in Work Sample (Content, Context, Cognition Types)	Alignment Comments: Curriculum	Alignment Comments: External First Assessed	Alignment Comments: External Assessment Grade Level
5/English Language Arts	14	One page written narrative; three paragraphs	In a one-page, three-paragraph essay using the guidelines from your writing lesson, relate a personal experience regarding a chore you had to complete, describing your work sequentially, and using transitions from paragraph to paragraph. Provide a conclusion that summarizes your evaluation of your performance of the chore and why you evaluated it as you did.	**Content:** Writing sequential narrative and drawing conclusion **Closest:** 4.6.23 ELA **Context:** Given a writing lesson emphasizing paragraphing and transitioning **Cognition types:** Knowledge, Application, and Evaluation	First tested on state assessment in grade 4.	Grade 5 state assessment requires more analysis than personal narratives; read a selection, consider the opposing ideas, and write a paragraph explaining the similarities and differences between them.
4/Social Studies	19	Map of state with large dots representing five cities and lines representing rivers	Label the cities indicated on the map by the large dots, and label the rivers represented by the lines.	**Content:** Know the locations of the largest cities and rivers in the state. **Closest:** 4.7.14 **Context:** Given lessons on cities and geographical features (rivers), recall and write …. **Cognition types:** Knowledge	Only rivers are tested and those are presented in multiple choices by map of the state, when tested at this grade level.	At grade level, the knowledge is tested with multiple choices for rivers; only two cities are included, and they are typically tested in multiple choice questions.

Assessment Implementation and Data Use

File Name	Content
Figure 3.40	Computer Generated Report
Figure 3.41	Hand Analysis: Math
Figure 3.42	Hand Analysis: Reading
Figure 3.43	Hand Analysis: Writing
Figure 3.44	Ten Tips for Effective Use of Data
Figure 3.45	Data Mentors

Figure 3.40 is a sample of data generated from machine-scored assessments. The format is user-friendly, so that teachers can easily identify objectives that are problematic.

Figure 3.41 shows how student progress can be tracked in situations where machine scoring is not feasible. The format of the recording sheet is based on the test specifications for mathematics found in Figure 3.32, another example of making documents work for multiple purposes to avoid duplication of efforts. Figure 3.41 also includes an example of how a simple hand-tally form might look when completed; the blank template is on the CD. The information on the tally sheet gives the classroom teacher immediate feedback on areas that need to be addressed for multiple students, while the individual scoring sheets provide individual student information.

Figure 3.42 is a simple form with two different ways of tracking reading progress—by individual students and by whole group.

Figure 3.43 is more extensive, tracking performance in all six traits of the Six-Trait Writing Model, which was developed by the Northwest Regional Educational Laboratory. Teachers could easily decide to focus on one trait on a specific grade level or over a certain length of time within a course.

Figure 3.44 is a list of tips for effective use of data. These tips can be used with both administrators and classroom teachers.

Figure 3.45 describes in outline form the goals of an ongoing data mentor program. A typical agenda for one training session is included on the CD.

MATHEMATICS DISTRICT ASSESSMENT: Class Item Analysis for Quarter 1

School: Happy Valley
Grade: 3
Teacher: 3C

Q. #	Objective #	Objective	Percent Correct		
			Class	School	District
1	102	Add whole numbers with carrying	94.7%	92.5%	89.6%
2	101	Add whole numbers	94.7%	92.5%	89.4%
3	101	Add whole numbers	84.2%	92.5%	92.2%
4	102	Add whole numbers with carrying	89.5%	92.5%	87.3%
5	111	Subtract whole numbers	100.0%	95.0%	91.2%
6	111	Subtract whole numbers	100.0%	97.5%	84.3%
7	112	Subtract whole numbers with borrowing	78.9%	80.0%	68.8%
8	112	Subtract whole numbers with borrowing	84.2%	90.0%	76.0%
9	24	Know by memory multiplication & division facts from 0x0 to 6x12	100.0%	97.5%	90.8%
10	24	Know by memory multiplication & division facts from 0x0 to 6x12	94.7%	95.0%	86.4%
11	60	Describe, extend, and explain the relationship in many kinds of patterns	100.0%	97.5%	94.3%
12	12	Counts by 10s or 100s starting with any number	100.0%	97.5%	84.8%
13	13	Express and interpret numbers up to four digits in expanded and standard form	68.4%	70.0%	47.7%
14	15	Use multiple representations for the same number	89.5%	82.0%	81.0%
15	20	Round four digit numbers to the nearest 10, 100, or 1,000	89.5%	92.5%	74.0%
16	21	Use front-end estimation in addition and subtraction of whole numbers	84.2%	90.0%	86.0%
17	46	Use geometric shapes to make other shapes by subdividing or combining	94.7%	82.5%	80.1%
18	3	Translate a number written as words (zero to one thousand) into numerals	94.7%	92.5%	84.6%
19	11	Use appropriate mathematical notation (<, >, =) to compare values	84.2%	80.0%	79.2%
20	61	Translate a written sentence into a number sentence	63.2%	77.5%	76.8%
21	63	Solve equations for missing factor in multiplication or division form	78.9%	72.5%	75.4%
22	62	Solve equations for missing addend or sum in addition or subtraction form	84.2%	80.0%	80.7%
23	62	Solve equations for missing addend or sum in addition or subtraction form	73.7%	80.0%	79.6%
24	63	Solve equations for missing factor in multiplication or division form	68.4%	67.5%	71.6%
25	1	Apply a variety of strategies to solve problems, including drawing a picture	78.8%	80.0%	76.2%

Note: Computation objectives have been subdivided for assessment purpose. Curriculum does *not* contain 112 objectives.

Figure 3.40

Figure 3.41

	Q1	Q2	Q3	Q4
Student: _Susie Queue_ **Total %**	70%			
Teacher: _Jones_ **Computation %**	60%			

3rd Grade—Test 1

Problem #	Objective	Descriptor	# Items	# Correct
1, 2, 3, 4, 5, 6, 30*	**3.2.1**	**Add/subtract whole numbers**	7	4
7, 8, 18	**3.2.5**	**Multiplication facts (2, 5, 10)**	3	2
9	3.1.7	Odd/even	1	1
10, 11	3.1.3	Represent numbers	2	2
12, 28*	3.1.2	Place value	2	0
13	3.1.5	Compare and arrange	1	0
14	3.1.1	Count, read, write numbers	1	1
15	3.1.4	Identify numbers from different combinations	1	1
16	3.2.7	Estimation	1	1
17, 21, 22, 29*	3.3.3	Operation symbols	4	3
19, 20	3.5.10b	Write money amounts	2	2
24	3.4.5	Congruent	1	0
23	3.4.7	Line segments and lines	1	1
25	3.4.8	Lines of symmetry	1	1
26, 27	3.5.9a	Time intervals and duration	2	1
		Total	30	20
		Computation	10	6

*Constructed response that addresses 3.6.1: Problem Solving. **Bold**=computation problems.

Figure 3.41

ITEM ANALYSIS SHEET

No. Students Tested: 20

Item	Number Missed	Percent Missed
1	/	5%
2	//	10%
3	/	5%
4	//	10%
5	/////	25%
6	/	5%
7		
8	//	10%
9		
10		
11		
12	////	20%
13	/	5%
14		
15		
16		
17		
18	/	5%
19		
20		
21		
22	///	15%
23		
24	//	10%
25	/	5%
26		
27	///////	35%
28	/	5%
29		
30	/	5%

Figure 3.42

READING PROGRESS CHART
Cash Elementary School

Percent Correct

Name	Narrative					Expository				
	Pre	Q #1	Q #2	Q #3	Post	Pre	Q #1	Q #2	Q #3	Post
Adams, John										
Backs, Green										
Card, Credit										
Cash, Cold H.										
Daynow, N. E.										
DuPont, Muni B.										
Fast, Buck										
Fatigable, N. D.										
Gold, Glittery										
Honest, Always										
Integrity, Soli D.										
Letter, I. Rhoda										
Pat, Stan										
Rogers, Buck										
Rooney, Annie										
Sample, Betty										
Sunshine, Ray F.										
Trustee, Ima										
Valiant, Ben										
Wishes, Beth										
Average										

Class Progress Chart

Score Range	Narrative									
	Pre-test		Quarter 1		Quarter 2		Quarter 3		Post-test	
	#	%	#	%	#	%	#	%	#	%
80-100										
60-79										
40-59										
20-39										
0-19										

SIX-TRAIT WRITING: SUMMARY DATA FOR PRACTICE ACTIVITIES

Step 1: Tally the number of students in your sample class who received each score on each trait on their practice papers.

October:

Trait → / Score ↓	Ideas		Organization		Voice		Word Choice		Sentence Fluency		Conventions	
	Tally	No.	Tally	No.	Tally	No.	Tally	No.	Tally	No.	Tally	No.
5												
4												
3												
2												
1												

November:

Trait → / Score ↓	Ideas		Organization		Voice		Word Choice		Sentence Fluency		Conventions	
	Tally	No.	Tally	No.	Tally	No.	Tally	No.	Tally	No.	Tally	No.
5												
4												
3												
2												
1												

Figure 3.43

Figure 3.44

Ten Tips for Using Data Effectively

1. Choose the right data.

2. Organize the data in a user-friendly manner.

3. Analyze it in a timely manner.

4. Make it available to all stakeholders.

5. Provide the staff development necessary to use data to inform decision-making.

6. Use data analysis to make programmatic changes.

7. Use data analysis to make instructional changes.

8. Use data analysis to determine student-specific interventions.

9. Design or select classroom and district assessments that are aligned with curriculum content.

10. Plan for the continuation of the process, both data delivery and staff development.

Figure 3.45

A DATA MENTORS PROGRAM

Purpose   Develop building capacity to organize, analyze, and use data

Structure   Regular meetings (monthly or bimonthly) with principals and two or three teachers per building

Content   Data notebook
Common vocabulary
Interpreting test results
Organizing and representing data
Looking at trend data
Building a school improvement plan
Developing and using performance assessments

Results   Increased knowledge and enthusiasm on the part of teachers and building administrators
Teacher-led data inservice in the buildings

Program Evaluation

File Name	Content
Figure 3.46	Program Evaluation Template
Figure 3.47	Sample Program Evaluation Plan and Related Documents
Figure 3.48	Executive Summary for Program Evaluation

Figure 3.46 is a template to guide the development of a program-evaluation action plan.

Figure 3.47 contains a partial program evaluation action plan in the book, with the completed plan on the CD. Actual student and parent surveys used in the evaluation are included in the sample on the CD.

Figure 3.48 in this book provides a single example of an executive summary, while the CD contains two. The additional executive summary on the CD corresponds to the program evaluation plan presented in Figure 3.47.

Figure 3.46

PROGRAM EVALUATION ACTION PLAN

Program to be evaluated:_____

I. PURPOSE

    A. Briefly describe the program to be evaluated. When was it initiated? How many schools, grades, or students are involved in the program?

    B. State the pre-existing goals or purposes of this program.

    C. What led to the decision to evaluate the program?

    D. What questions do you expect to answer in conducting this evaluation?

II. PARAMETERS

    A. Describe the scope of this evaluation. (Is it district, building, or grade level?)

    B. What timeframe will the evaluation cover?

    C. What components of the program will be evaluated? (These might include student achievement, personnel, staff development, curriculum scope and sequence, and/or instructional materials.)

III. PROCESS

Provide a detailed management plan that includes the following:

    A. Personnel needed to conduct the evaluation, with assigned responsibilities

    B. Data (quantitative or qualitative) that will be gathered, method of analysis, and criteria for determining program strengths and weaknesses

    C. Resources required, including budget requirements

    D. Timeline for entire process

    E. Plans for communicating results and recommendations.

IV. FOLLOW-UP

    A. Give a brief description of follow-up plans for the year following the evaluation report.

    B. Submit a report at the end of one year to describe follow-up activities.

Figure 3.47

PROGRAM EVALUATION ACTION PLAN

Program to be evaluated: <u>Sample High School Police Academy</u>

I. PURPOSE

A. Briefly describe the program to be evaluated. When was it initiated? How many schools, grades, or students are involved in the program?

The Sample High School Police Academy Magnet is one of several thematic programs at Sample High that implement a school-within-a-school approach. The efficacy of this approach has strong research support; the research data indicate that smaller schools within a larger school result in a sense of community among the students and increased academic achievement.

The mission statement of the Sample High School Police Academy reads, in part, as follows: "By providing a rigorous academic high school curriculum, the Sample High School Police Academy Magnet School prepares highly motivated young men and women for careers in law enforcement and other related fields."

While a specific goal of the Police Academy Magnet is to assist students with successful completion of A-G requirements, Academy faculty must also address specialized curriculum requirements. Literature-based units in English are expected to provide the opportunity to discuss ethics and legal and cultural issues. Science must include forensic science, students must develop knowledge of how computer hardware and software are used in law enforcement, and a high level of physical fitness is required as part of the physical education program. Coordinating both sets of requirements provides a challenge for Academy staff.

B. State the pre-existing goals or purposes of this program.

The goals of the program are as follows:
- Promote interest in a law enforcement career.
- Assist students in successful completion of the A-G requirements.
- Develop a strong sense of community involvement (20-hour/semester community involvement requirement).
- Increase post-secondary enrollment of Police Academy graduates.

C. What led to the decision to evaluate the program?

During the 2000-2001 school year, external evaluators visited Sample High School under the IIUSP program. One of the recommendations in the final report of those evaluators was to establish a program evaluation procedure and a timeline for evaluating the multitude of programs that exist at the school. The evaluation of the Policy Academy Magnet is one of the first evaluations to be conducted. It was chosen because it impacts a fairly large number of students.

Figure 3.48

EXECUTIVE SUMMARY
Program Evaluation
Midwest High School Two-Year Algebra I Program
April 2004

Introduction

A two-year Algebra I sequence was introduced at Midwest High in the fall of 2001. The following measurable goals were established for the program:
- Reduce the failure rate in all mathematics classes, with special attention to Algebra I.
- Increase the enrolment in classes above Algebra I, specifically Geometry and Algebra II.
- Reduce enrollment in Math 1 and Math 2.

Data Collection

Data were collected by the following methods:
- Analysis of failing grades at the end of each semester,
- Analysis of total enrollment, based on Sept. 20 official counts, and
- Analysis of subsequent enrollment and grades of students completing Algebra 1B in the spring of 2003

Analysis of Failures

Failures from first semester of the 2000-01 school year provide baseline data. Second semester failures for 2000-01 were not recorded. Based on six semesters of data related to failures, the following observations can be made.
- Total failures across time have fluctuated very little. Second semester failures tend to be higher than first semester failures. First semester failures for the current year (10 percent) were higher than for the previous two years.
- The percent of failures in the yearlong Algebra 1 course have decreased between 2000 and 2003, while failures in the Algebra 1A and 1B courses have increased consistently.
- The total percent of failures in all Algebra 1 courses (Algebra 1, Algebra 1A, and Algebra 1B) has remained fairly stable. Declines for 2001-02 and 2002-03 were offset by an increase in 2003-2004.

Enrollment

- Enrollment in Math 1-Math 3 has declined from 17 percent of all math enrollment in the fall of 2000 to just 8 percent of all math enrollment in the fall of 2003.
- Total Algebra I enrollment has increased from 22 percent of all math enrollment in 2000 to 30 percent of all math enrollment in 2003.
- The percent of total math enrollment in Algebra 1 or below is relatively unchanged, 39 percent in 2000 compared with 38 percent in 2003.
- Enrollment in Geometry, which would have first been affected in the fall of 2003, has declined from 18 percent to 15 percent.
- There has not been sufficient time for this program to impact Algebra II enrollment. However, a decline in Geometry enrollment in the current year may be a predictor of a decline in Algebra II enrollment next year.

Success of Students Completing Alg. 1B

- Of 57 students who completed Algebra 1B in the spring of 2003, 33 (60 percent) took Geometry in the fall of 2003.
- Of those 33 students, only one received a grade higher than a C, while the remainder received a grade lower than a C.
- Thirty percent of students entering Geometry from Algebra 1B received F's first semester of 2000, compared with 10 percent of all Geometry students.

Figure 3.48

Conclusions
The Algebra 1A/1B program is successfully meeting its goal of reducing the number of students enrolled in Math 1, Math 2, and Math 3.

Failure rate of students in the Algebra 1A/1B sequence is lower than the failure rate in Math 1, but higher than the failure rate of the yearlong Algebra 1 class.

The program did not increase enrollment in Geometry in the current year, which was the first year that impact could be measured.

Students who moved on to Geometry from the Algebra 1A/1B sequence did not have a successful experience. Very few, if any, can be expected to move on to a successful experience in Algebra 2.

Recommendations
Building and district administrators and math faculty at Midwest High School need to carefully review the data to determine if this sequence of courses should be continued.

Glossary

Most of us hear educational terms that sound familiar to us, and we readily draw our own definitions from the contexts in which we have previously heard them. It is not uncommon to learn subsequently that the intended meaning was quite different from our own understanding. Additionally, the same term often carries different meaning or implication from state to state and district to district. To alleviate any confusion on the part of users of this practitioners' guide, the following definitions are provided to clarify the authors' meanings of terms used in this text and to offer alternative terminology where it might be helpful to do so.

Alignment – generally referring to parallelism and congruence among written, taught, and tested curriculum; specific applications include the following:

> alignment in curriculum design – refers to the parallelism and congruence between assessments in which students are asked to demonstrate knowledge or skills and the guidance to instruction contained in the local curriculum documents
>
> alignment in curriculum delivery – refers to parallelism and congruence between the teachers' instructional activities and the learning objectives outlined in the written curriculum
>
> alignment levels – topical (simple parallelism of topics addressed in written, taught, and tested curriculum) or deep alignment (parallelism that also includes the various contextual ways students learn the objective and how they are asked to demonstrate the knowledge or skills)

Articulation – the logical progression of learning objectives from grade level to grade level or from course to course within the curricular content areas, the connectivity of learning that creates seamless learning through the student's educational experience; articulation teaming means involving teachers from multiple grade levels to collaborate on implementing curriculum in ways that enhance the intended articulation

Backloading – an approach to curriculum design that begins with analysis of what students are expected to know or be able to do as derived from externally (usually state level) prescribed assessments or standards, as compared with frontloading

Benchmark – a designated expectation of student learning at a particular point in the curriculum sequence

Bloom's taxonomy – a classification of learning skills based on Benjamin Bloom's studies of the cognitive domain, refers to types of cognition that range from knowledge through evaluation; often referred to as levels of cognition but not always linear

Cognition – the mental processes, the types or levels of thinking and learning; most frequently referring to those elements of Bloom's taxonomy (Knowledge, Comprehension, Application, Analysis, Synthesis, Evaluation)

Concept – an underlying principle or broad category of learning

Content – in curriculum design, refers to the specific learning objective(s) within the subject area, the "what" of the learning

Context – in curriculum design and delivery, refers to the ways in which a specific learning objective is approached, the conditions surrounding the learning, "how" the students will learn and demonstrate their learning of the objective

Criterion-referenced tests – (CRT's) tests that are designed in specific alignment with district curriculum objectives and identified criteria for assessing the intended skill or knowledge that a student has mastered; not a measurement of students' mastery in comparison with other students, but a measurement against established criteria

Curriculum guides – refers to local district documents that direct the breadth (scope) and order (sequence) of curriculum at all grade levels within a given content area and provide supporting information for teachers regarding instructional materials to be used, supplemental materials needed, assessment strategies and linkage with required state or district tests (or other high-stakes assessments such as SAT or ACT), and ideas for classroom activities that lead to mastery of the local curriculum objectives derived from state expectations

Curriculum management – refers to the system and processes for design, delivery, monitoring, evaluation, and review of curriculum over time; includes designation of roles and responsibilities and timelines and focuses on curriculum design, materials selection, training/staff development, implementation, assessment of progress, and program evaluation

Data-based (or data-driven) decisions – decisions made after analysis and consideration of information such as attendance, test scores, grades, surveys, program evaluations, and similar compilations of objective information (sometimes accompanied by interpretive reports)

Delivery – refers to implementation of curriculum; the instruction or instructional practices entailed in implementing the curriculum in the classrooms

Design – refers to the writing, documentation of curriculum or assessments; the written intent, as preliminary to or different from the delivery or implementation

Development – the broad process incorporating several steps, procedures, or components (e.g., curriculum development)

Disaggregation – refers to the breakdown of assessment data by specific factors such as school, grade level, gender, ethnicity, socio-economic factors, or length of time within the district; refinement of data specificity to enable use of the information at the school and classroom levels as well as in district-level contexts

Formative – as in "formative assessments;" refers to ongoing types of quizzes, tests, discussions, or similar methods of checking the students' mastery of objectives in the curriculum primarily to guide teacher decisions regarding review, reteaching, or proceeding to new objectives

Frontloading – an approach to curriculum design that begins with local determination of what students should know or be able to do, as compared with backloading, and builds curriculum from those decisions

Goal – broad statement of the intended outcome of the student learning, usually accompanied by a series of more precise statements of learning expectations that are commonly referred to as objectives

Implementation – carrying out, putting into action the agreed upon or approved plan, curriculum, or assessment; follow-up use of an intended practice

Indicator – a piece of information or a statistic that gives feedback regarding progress toward specific goals and skills

Instructional materials – the textbooks, software programs, and other resources to be used in delivery of the curriculum. (See primary and supplemental instructional materials)

Inter-rater reliability – consistency of results among those persons performing the same evaluation tasks using the same rubrics or criteria so that evaluations of the same subject (e.g., documents) are likely to be the same from rater to rater at any given time; important to the fair and appropriate scoring of anything being evaluated by multiple raters

Mastery – accomplishment of the intended learning as expressed in the objectives at the level of performance expected, usually referring to such accomplishment as prerequisite to forward movement into the next learning

Measurable objective – an objective worded in such a way that the mastery of it can be demonstrated or quantified by level of accuracy

Monitoring – oversight and coaching of curriculum implementation, assigned primarily to school administrators but sometimes assisted by various other district staff or teacher teams

Needs assessment – a process to gather information regarding factors that should influence decisions about educational program planning and curriculum; typically includes research, program evaluations and student assessment data, local demographic and economic information, expectations from internal (district, community) and external (state, federal) sources

Objective – the "what" of student learning, refers to the statement of what the student is expected to know or be able to do in the subject area, usually at a specific grade level; sometimes also referred to as a learning indicator, mastery indicator, learning target, benchmark, or other similar terms, depending on the state or district in which the terminology is used

Outcomes – results, goals of curriculum, instruction, and student learning

Pacing guides – documents designed to present a "map" for implementing the curriculum in a given grade level or course; contains broadly estimated calendar and time allocations for learning objectives, clusters of objectives, units, or similar organizational components

Piloting – refers to the "practice run" or "trial run" of implementing a draft curriculum and proposed instructional materials for the curriculum, or of administering a draft set of district assessments; the preliminary implementation usually involving a sample of grade levels or one section of each grade level (or course levels at the secondary schools)

Primary instructional materials – those materials approved for use by all teachers in conjunction with teaching of the approved curriculum

Program evaluation – an organized set of procedures to gather information regarding the effectiveness of a program based on various data sources

Rubrics – a set of criteria describing performance at different levels of quality for the intended learning, project, or activity; includes a definition of the requirement for a rating score of a specific level

Scope and sequence – refers to the documentation of learning goals and objectives within a subject area organized in the order in which they are to be mastered by grade level; the curriculum informational foundation upon which curriculum guides are built

Self-reflective – describes the approach to thinking about and reviewing one's own behaviors and skills in the context of improving teachers' instruction and student results, as compared with supervisor-generated evaluative or judgmental direction

Spiraling – vertical progression of related content learning objectives that includes periodic revisiting of some topics or content over several years and addressing them in greater complexity and depth at each visit

Standard – a broadly stated expectation of student learning that serves as the basis for a related cluster of more specific required learnings (objectives, learning targets, benchmarks) necessary to meet the broad expectation; content and performance standards – statements like goals and objectives telling what students should know and be able to do

Summative – as in "summative assessments," refers to final exams, end-of-course or end-of-grade-level district tests, state assessments at ends of specified periods of time in the learning related to state standards

Supplemental materials – those instructional materials that can be used either to fill in the gaps for curriculum areas not adequately addressed in the primary materials or to enhance or extend the learning beyond the content of the primary materials

Suggestions for Further Reading

Bloom, Benjamin, ed. *Taxonomy Of Educational Objectives: Cognitive Domain.* Boston, MA: Allyn and Bacon, 1956.

Downey, Carolyn, Betty Steffy, Larry Frase, Fenwick English, and William Poston. *The Three-Minute Classroom Walk-Through: Changing School Supervisory Practice One Teacher At A Time.* Thousand Oaks, CA: Corwin Press, 2004.

English, Fenwick. *Curriculum Management for Schools, Colleges, and Business.* Springfield, IL: Charles C. Thomas, 1987.

English, Fenwick. *Deciding What to Teach and Test: Developing, Aligning, and Auditing the Curriculum.* (Millennium edition) Thousand Oaks, CA: Corwin Press, 2000.

English, Fenwick, and Betty Steffy. *Deep Curriculum Alignment: Creating a Level Playing Field for All Children on High-Stakes Tests of Educational Accountability.* Lanham, MD: Scarecrow Press, Inc., 2001.

Frase, Larry, Fenwick English, and William Poston, eds. *Curriculum Auditing.* Lancaster, PA: Technomic Publishing Co., 1995.

Marzano, Robert. *What Works in Schools: Translating Research into Action.* Alexandria, VA: ASCD, 2003.

Marzano, Robert, Debra Pickering, and Jane Pollack. *Classroom Instruction that Works.* Alexandria, VA: ASCD, 2002.

Reeves, Douglas. *101 Questions and Answers about Standards, Assessment, and Accountability.* Denver, CO: Advanced Learning Press, 2001.

Sanders, James. *Evaluating School Programs: An Educator's Guide* (2nd edition). Thousands Oaks, CA: Corwin Press, 2000.

Schmoker, Michael. *Results: The Key To Continuous School Improvement* (2nd edition). Alexandria, VA; ASCD, 1999.

Steffy, Betty. *Curriculum Alignment: A Facilitator's Guide to Deciding What to Teach and Test.* Thousand Oaks, CA: Corwin Press, 1999.

Stiggins, Richard J. *Student-Centered Classroom Assessment* (2nd edition). Upper Saddle River, NJ; Prentice-Hall, Inc., 1997.

Tomlinson, Carol. *The Differentiated Classroom: Responding to the Needs of All Learners.* Alexandria, VA: ASCD, 1999.

USEFUL WEB SITE LINKS

The following Web sites are offered as possible links to information and resources for educational leaders and practitioners. Several of the sites provide direct links to additional and more specialized sources.

Source	Web sites
Achieve Inc.	www.achieve.org
American Educational Research Association	www.aera.net
American Association of School Librarians	www.ala.org/aasl
American Library Association	www.ala.org
Annenburg Institute for School Reform	www.annenburginstitute.org
Association for Supervision & Curriculum Development	www.ascd.org
Brookings Institution	www.brook.edu
Center for Educational Reform	www.edreform.com
Center for Research on Education, Diversity & Excellence	www.crede.ucsc.edu
Center for the Improvement of Early Reading Achievement	www.ciera.org
Council for Exceptional Children	www.cec.sped.org
Council of Chief State School Officers	www.ccsso.org
Council of the Great City Schools	www.cgcs.org
Education Commission of the States	www.ecs.org
Educational Research Service	www.ers.org
Educational Resources Information Center	www.eric.ed.gov
Learning First Alliance	www.learningfirst.org
National Alliance of Black School Educators	www.nabse.org
National Assessment of Educational Progress	www.ed.gov/programs/naep
National Association for Multicultural Education	www.nameorg.org
National Association of Elementary School Principals	www.naesp.org
National Association of Secondary School Principals	www.nasspcms.principals.org
National Association of State Boards of Education	www.nasbe.org
National Center for Education Information	www.ncei.com
National Center for Educational Accountability	www.nc4ea.org
National Center for Improving Student Learning and Achievement in Mathematics and Science	www.wcer.wisc.edu/ncisla
National Center for Research on Evaluation, Standards, and Student Testing	www.csd.uda.edu
National Council of Teachers of English	www.ncte.org
National Council of Teachers of Mathematics	www.nctm.org
National Science Teachers Association	www.nsta.org
National Council for Social Studies	www.ncss.org
National Educational Service	www.nesonline.com

National Educational Technology Standards	http://cnets.iste.org
National Research Center on English Learning and Achievement	www.cela.albany.edu
National Research Center on the Gifted and Talented	www.ed.gov/offices/OER
National School Boards Association	www.nsba.org
Office of Educational Research & Improvement (USDOE)	www.ed.gov/offices/OERI
Phi Delta Kappa International	www.pdkintl.org
RAND Education	www.rand.org/centers/education
The Education Trust	www2.edtrust.org
The Gateway to Educational Material	www.thegateway.org
The Thomas B. Fordham Foundation	www.edexcellence.net
U.S. Department of Education	www.ed.gov

The authors and publishers of this book offer no endorsement of or assume no liability for the currency, accuracy, or availability of information on the sites listed here.

Index

About the Authors

Beverly W. Nichols, Ph.D.

Beverly Nichols is an independent education consultant assisting schools and school systems in many areas of school improvement. She recently served as the Coordinator of Evaluation and Assessment and Resource Specialist for Secondary Mathematics and Computer Science in Shawnee Mission, Kansas Public Schools. She has more than 40 years of experience in mathematics education and educational leadership, including administrative roles at the junior and senior high school levels and in curriculum and assessment. Her classroom teaching experience has included elementary and high school classes, as well as college level courses in computer programming and mathematics education. She has worked as a consultant with textbook companies and school districts across several states, providing assistance with staff development, curriculum and assessment development, data analysis, and school improvement plans.

Dr. Nichols received her B.A. and M.A. from Arizona State University, an Ed.S. in Educational Administration from Emporia State University, and a Ph.D. in curriculum and instruction from the University of Missouri at Kansas City. She completed her curriculum audit management training in Bloomington, Indiana and San Antonio, Texas in 1997. She has participated in audits or external evaluations in 14 states. She is also a certified Classroom Walk-Through trainer and has led administrators in that training in numerous locations.

Dr. Nichols is a recipient of the Presidential Award for Excellence in Teaching Mathematics and has served on the Board of Directors, as well as many committees for the National Council of Teachers of Mathematics. She has been a presenter at numerous regional and national meetings of mathematics teachers across the United States and in Canada. She has written for *The Mathematics Teacher*, a journal of the National Council of Teachers of Mathematics, and served as editor for a special issue of the journal.

Dr. Nichols has worked extensively with Phi Delta Kappa to assist rural schools in southern Indiana in the alignment of their local curriculum and assessments to Indiana state standards. As part of this work, she led the planning and implementation of four one-week summer workshops in curriculum and assessment that were attended by almost 300 Indiana teachers and administrators. In addition, under the auspices of PDK, she has conducted data mentoring workshops in Arizona, California, Georgia, Kansas, and Oklahoma. She and Dr. Kevin Singer co-authored an article on data mentoring for ASCD's *Educational Leadership*.

Sue Shidaker, M.Ed.

Sue Shidaker is currently an education consultant with services incorporated as Riverside Educational Consultants, Inc. located in Cincinnati, Ohio. Her primary work consists of professional development, facilitation of team-building and planning processes, analysis and drafting of public policy, and assisting school districts in areas of curriculum, assessment, and school improvement. She also leads and serves on Curriculum Management Audit teams for Curriculum Management Systems, Inc. and Phi Delta Kappa and provides training in Classroom Walk-Throughs and Curriculum Alignment, strategies designed to help improve student learning and achievement.

Ms. Shidaker's education career has included classroom teaching and administration at the junior and senior high school levels, as well as district-level administration in finance/operations, curriculum/educational programs, and human resources.

Ms. Shidaker has also served as president of a local school board and president of a state school boards association. Subsequently, she was a special assistant to the governor of Alaska for policy areas including, among others, K-12 and postsecondary education. Her state government experience also included responsibilities as deputy commissioner for the state department of administration and service on the Western Interstate Commission on Higher Education.

Ms. Shidaker was a Lead External Evaluator with the California Curriculum Management Audit Center for the state's Immediate Intervention for Under-performing Schools Program and now leads individual school audits, based on the original California model. She is the author of two chapters in the text *The Curriculum Management Audit: Improving School Quality,* various education articles, and handbooks related to local and state governmental processes.

Sue completed her B.A. degree in French and English at Ohio Wesleyan University and her M.Ed. in education administration at the University of Alaska, Anchorage. She completed additional graduate work at The Ohio State University, Duke University, Arizona State University, and Seattle Pacific University. Sue received her curriculum audit training in Missouri in 1988 and has led audits and participated on audit teams in 23 states since then.

Kevin Singer, Ed.D.

Dr. Kevin Singer is currently the Superintendent of Schools for the Manheim Township School District in Lancaster, Pennsylvania. Prior to this position he held positions as Superintendent of Schools in the Grapevine-Colleyville Independent School District in Texas and the Associate Superintendent for Curriculum and Instruction in Shawnee Mission, Kansas. During his professional career, he has served at the district administration level as a building principal and as a teacher in both middle and elementary schools.

Dr. Singer received his B.A. at Washburn University in Topeka, Kansas. He earned both his master's degree and his doctorate at the University of Kansas. Dr. Singer leads and serves on Curriculum Management Audit teams for Curriculum Management Systems, Inc. and Phi Delta Kappa and has participated in more than 20 audits across the United States. He has served as consultant to the Ministries of Education in Moscow, Russia and Bermuda. With Dr. Beverly Nichols, he co-authored an article on data mentoring for ASCD's *Educational Leadership.*

Gene Johnson, Ed.D.

Dr. Gene Johnson is currently the Associate Superintendent for Secondary Administration in the Shawnee Mission School District in the metropolitan Kansas City area. Previously he served as Associate Superintendent for Educational Services, Director of Elementary Programs, and an elementary principal in Shawnee Mission. He also served as a teacher and building administrator in Topeka Public Schools and in North Topeka school districts.

Dr. Johnson's experiences include extensive work in effective instruction, school improvement, and system planning. He has been directly responsible for curriculum and instruction, special education, and career education departments in a school district of 30,000 students. Dr. Johnson also has extensive experience in the area of personnel evaluation.

Dr. Johnson is a certified Classroom Walk-Through trainer, has participated in Phi Delta Kappa trainings for Indiana school corporations, and serves as a senior lead auditor and national trainer for Curriculum Management Systems, Inc. He has served as a lead auditor or audit team member on 18 curriculum management audits throughout the United States.

Dr. Johnson received his B.A. from Yankton College, South Dakota; his M.A. degree from Washburn University in Topeka, Kansas; and his Ed. D. in educational policy and administration from the University of Kansas.